ALTERNATIVE REALITIES

QUICK TAKES: MOVIES AND POPULAR CULTURE

Quick Takes: Movies and Popular Culture is a series offering succinct overviews and high quality writing on cutting edge themes and issues in film studies. Authors offer both fresh perspectives on new areas of inquiry and original takes on established topics.

SERIES EDITORS:

Gwendolyn Audrey Foster is Willa Cather Professor of English and teaches film studies in the Department of English at the University of Nebraska, Lincoln.

Wheeler Winston Dixon is the James Ryan Endowed Professor of Film Studies and professor of English at the University of Nebraska, Lincoln.

Rebecca Bell-Metereau,
Transgender Cinema

Blair Davis,
Comic Book Movies

Jonna Eagle,
War Games

Lester D. Freidman,
Sports Movies

Desirée J. Garcia,
The Movie Musical

Steven Gerrard,
The Modern British Horror Film

Barry Keith Grant,
Monster Cinema

Julie Grossman,
The Femme Fatale

Daniel Herbert,
Film Remakes and Franchises

Ian Olney, *Zombie Cinema*

Valérie K. Orlando,
New African Cinema

Carl Plantinga,
Alternative Realities

Stephen Prince,
Digital Cinema

Dahlia Schweitzer,
L.A. Private Eyes

Steven Shaviro,
Digital Music Videos

David Sterritt,
Rock 'n' Roll Movies

John Wills, *Disney Culture*

Alternative Realities

CARL PLANTINGA

RUTGERS UNIVERSITY PRESS

New Brunswick, Camden, and Newark, New Jersey, and London

Library of Congress Cataloging-in-Publication Data
Names: Plantinga, Carl, author.
Title: Alternative realities / Carl Plantinga.
Description: New Brunswick : Rutgers University Press, 2020. |
Series: Quick takes: movies and popular culture |
Includes bibliographical references and index.
Identifiers: LCCN 2020008408 | ISBN 9780813599816 (paperback) |
ISBN 9780813599823 (hardcover) | ISBN 9780813599830 (epub) |
ISBN 9780813599847 (mobi) | ISBN 9780813599854 (pdf)
Subjects: LCSH: Realism in motion pictures. | Fantasy in motion
pictures. | Motion pictures—Technological innovations.
Classification: LCC PN1995.9.R3 P53 | DDC 791.43/612—dc23
LC record available at https://lccn.loc.gov/2020008408

A British Cataloging-in-Publication record for this book is
available from the British Library.

∞ The paper used in this publication meets the requirements of
the American National Standard for Information Sciences—
Permanence of Paper for Printed Library Materials,
ANSI Z39.48-1992.

www.rutgersuniversitypress.org

Manufactured in the United States of America

Alternative Realities

CARL PLANTINGA

RUTGERS UNIVERSITY PRESS

New Brunswick, Camden, and Newark, New Jersey, and London

Library of Congress Cataloging-in-Publication Data
Names: Plantinga, Carl, author.
Title: Alternative realities / Carl Plantinga.
Description: New Brunswick : Rutgers University Press, 2020. |
Series: Quick takes: movies and popular culture |
Includes bibliographical references and index.
Identifiers: LCCN 2020008408 | ISBN 9780813599816 (paperback) |
ISBN 9780813599823 (hardcover) | ISBN 9780813599830 (epub) |
ISBN 9780813599847 (mobi) | ISBN 9780813599854 (pdf)
Subjects: LCSH: Realism in motion pictures. | Fantasy in motion
pictures. | Motion pictures—Technological innovations.
Classification: LCC PN1995.9.R3 P53 | DDC 791.43/612—dc23
LC record available at https://lccn.loc.gov/2020008408

A British Cataloging-in-Publication record for this book is
available from the British Library.

∞ The paper used in this publication meets the requirements of
the American National Standard for Information Sciences—
Permanence of Paper for Printed Library Materials,
ANSI Z39.48-1992.

www.rutgersuniversitypress.org

Manufactured in the United States of America

CONTENTS

ALTERNATIVE REALITIES

INTRODUCTION

Much of the fun of watching *Guardians of the Galaxy Vol. 2* (2017) is marveling at the fantastical world and characters thought up by the filmmakers. Aside from the very human-looking Peter Quill (Chris Pratt), makeup and digital artists present us with a diverse group, from the green-skinned Gamora (Zoe Saldana) and blue-skinned, crooked-toothed Yondo Udanta (Michael Rooker) to Gamora's blue-gray cyborg sister Nebula to Baby Groot, the odd combination of tree sapling and human infant, and finally, to Rocket, a genetically engineered bounty hunter and mercenary who looks much like a terrestrial raccoon. These Guardians of the Galaxy travel through dozens of fantastical worlds populated by bizarre landscapes and outlandish creatures. The story even features a god, Ego (Kurt Russell), with his very own planet. This god at one point morphs into the television star David Hasselhoff, but this is nothing compared to the fantastical changes to his planet itself. The spectacular interior of Ego's planet was inspired by the fractal art of Hal Tenny and was designed to be extremely geometrical, employing many fractals, including Apollonian gaskets.

This is a book about the imaginary worlds created in the medium of motion pictures. But it is also about the nature of this expressive and powerful medium. The movies are capable of producing mind-blowing fantastical worlds and characters. The very perceptual basis of film is rooted in illusion, since the illusion of movement results from a series of still images, projected in succession, that trick our eyes and brains into seeing something moving on the screen. The capacity of the medium for fantasy and the fantastic was recognized by the earliest practitioners. In the late nineteenth and early twentieth centuries, the French filmmaker and magician Georges Méliès, in films such as *A Trip to the Moon* (1902) and *The Kingdom of the Fairies* (1903), used stop-motion cinematography and whimsical sets and costumes to create bizarre worlds and impossible events. The rise of sophisticated digital technologies in the past decades, often combined with traditional makeup, costume, sets, and the like, has resulted in a resurgence of popular animated fantasy, superhero, and science-fiction films on the big screen, many of which present strange and imaginative alternative worlds.

One the other hand, however, the film medium has been characterized as realist, as having a unique and powerful capacity to reveal the *objective* world with a compelling power unequaled by any other representational medium. Some of the earliest projected films—those of the Lumière brothers in France in the late nineteenth century—were basically the world's first home movies, designed simply to record an event occurring in front of the camera. This realist tradition continues today in both the documentary and the fiction film. After viewing Debra Granik's realist fiction films *Winter's Bone* (2010) or *Leave No Trace* (2017), the viewer is left with a sense that the films provide an authentic approximation of life among meth manufacturers in the Ozarks or, in the latter film, what it might be like to live off the grid in the forests of Oregon.

More than this sense of objective realism, however, the movies are also capable of representing the *subjective* experience of the world. Thinkers as diverse as the psychologists Oliver Sacks, Williams James, and Hugo Munsterberg and the film theorist V. F. Perkins have pointed out that movies are particularly capable of representing individual human experience (Plantinga, *Moving* 48–49). Perkins likened the movie medium to a "mind recorder" (133); it would be more accurate to call it an "experience recorder." What might it be like, as a young woman, to marry a wealthy widower and move into his imposing mansion by the sea, then to be haunted by the creepy specter of his deceased wife? What might it be like to volunteer to marry a Nazi in service of the CIA and your country, then realize that the man and his frightening mother have discovered your identity and have been gradually poisoning you? Watch Alfred Hitchcock's films *Rebecca* (1940) and *Notorious* (1946) to find out. A movie does not typically describe the experience (although verbal description through dialogue and/or voice-over narration is an option, of course) but typically provides the phenomenology of the experience—how it sounds, looks, and feels. It presents the spectator with images and sounds that often have a direct sensuous effect that resonates through the body and mind.

Alternative Realities explores the complex intersection between reality and fantasy, subjective and objective representation, in the movies. It examines the complexities inherent in a medium that can record what is in front of the camera, on the one hand, and provide nearly limitless avenues for the creative expression of the human imagination, on the other. *Alternative Realities* describes the nature of "world making" in movies and suggests some of the important ways that spectators are cued to respond to those worlds. It shows that even the most surreal fantasies ground their images, sounds, and narratives, to a large extent, in quotidian reality. On the other hand, it also shows that even the most realistic documentaries and realist fictional styles rely on creative structures that are products of the human imagination rather than mere imitations of the outside world. As the French film theorist Jean Mitry writes, the movies break down the barrier between fantasy and reality. In the same way that the medium "'injects fantasy' into reality, so it 'injects reality' into fantasy" (363). This combination of realism and imagination, of the objective and the subjective, the book argues, is a key to the expressive and psychological power of movies, and that power makes considerations of ethics vitally important. Ultimately, this book is a meditation on the capacity of movies to extend the human imagination but remain grounded in everyday reality. It also reveals the means by which movies can correspond with the world around us and have the capacity to educate, illuminate, and inspire through a combination of realist and expressive technique.

Chapter 1, "Realism and the Imagination," surveys what has been said and written about movie realism or, in other words, about the relationship between movies and the real world. Chapter 2, "Fantasy and Reality," examines what is thought to be reality's opposite—fantasy—and surveys some of the latest technologies used to create fantastical worlds and characters. A look at Patty Jenkins's *Wonder Woman* (2017) and James Gunn's *Guardians of the Galaxy* (2014) not only highlights the imaginative capacities of the medium but also demonstrates that all popular fantasies remain firmly rooted in the subjective human experience of the world. Chapter 3, "Subjective Realities," explores the capacity of movies to represent highly subjective experiences especially during bizarre or heightened states of mind and body. In examining films such as Christopher Nolan's *Memento* (2000), Michel Gondry's *Eternal Sunshine of the Spotless Mind* (2004), Joel and Ethan Coen's *The Big Lebowski* (1998), and Nolan's *Inception* (2010), the chapter focuses on the representation of memories and dreams.

Chapter 4, "Ruptured Realities," focuses on Martin Scorsese's *Shutter Island* (2010), Lana and Lilly Wachowski's *The Matrix* (1999), Franklin J. Schaffner's *Planet of the Apes* (1968), and similar films that undermine our epistemic certainty. These are movies that gradually disclose hidden worlds, that posit worlds within worlds, or that provide surprise endings that challenge everything we had previously assumed. These are the twist endings and "frame shifters," screen stories that alter a previous frame of reference and throw viewers into serious doubt. The chapter ends with a discussion of the ethics of such films that challenge our assumptions.

Chapter 5, "Documentary: The Art of Reality?," examines the documentary and similar forms, including what is popularly called the "mockumentary." The complicated relationship between movies and reality does not end with the fiction film. This chapter shows that although documentaries are sometimes called the "art of the real," they nonetheless employ all sorts of creative techniques that are shared with fictional moviemaking. All documentaries are the product of the human imagination, not a mere record of whatever was in front of the camera. This chapter reflects on the differences between fictions and documentaries in regard to their relationship to the actual world. The chapter examines the nature of docudrama, a kind of filmmaking that seems to mix elements of fiction and nonfiction, such that spectators are sometimes unsure about how to relate them to the historical record. Using the classic mock documentary Rob Reiner's *This Is Spinal Tap* (1976) as an example, the chapter also explores these "fake" documentaries that wear the mantle of documentary ironically. Mock documentaries, I argue, are fiction films ironically posing as documentaries.

The argument of the book is that the movies enact a dance between the creative, fantastical possibilities of the medium and its groundedness in the everyday world and our experience of it. The moving image is a composite medium, using a variety of communicative techniques that sometimes have striking correspondences to our world and experience of it but that are always used for some expressive or rhetorical purpose. To better understand the relationship between realism and fantasy, the subjective and objective, and fiction and nonfiction is to better understand the medium and its possibilities and the power of films to move us and influence cultures. Finally, it should be noted that all dates for the films mentioned in this text are from the Internet Movie Data Base; all box-office figures are from Box Office Mojo.

1

REALISM AND
THE IMAGINATION

When August and Louis Lumière held their first screening of projected motion pictures in 1895 in Paris, they had little idea of the potential of the movie medium. In fact, the brothers saw the movies as a mere novelty and withdrew from the business in 1905. During their time in the fledgling movie industry, however, the brothers' employees screened their brief films around the world and to great acclaim. Audiences were enthralled by the novelty—photographic pictures that seemed to move! that bore the stamp of reality! Most of these films were recordings of family life, urban scenes, ceremonies and parades, and similar everyday events. They were often filmed in one take from a single vantage point and with an unmoving camera. Among these 1895 movies are *Workers Leaving the Lumière Factory, The Baby's Snack, The Sea (Bathing in the Sea),* and *The Blacksmiths.*

Still photography had been around since the early nineteenth century, so audiences were familiar with "the pencil of nature," as the pioneer photographer and inventor William Henry Fox Talbot called it. The novelty of *moving* pictures, of course, was the movement. The movies not only offered photographic pictures that seemed realistic and reliable but also made them move, as though one were witnessing life itself parade by on the screen. Audiences could see children jumping into the sea for a swim, babies being fed, snowball fights, and ostriches marching through the streets of Paris. Like the still camera, the motion-picture camera was a machine and thus seemingly capable of capturing and recording reality, to a certain extent, without the subjective input of the cinematographer. Making a moving photographic image is in part a mechanical process. The cinematographer need only set the camera up and point it, find the correct exposure, focus the lens, run the unexposed film through the camera, process the exposed film, and—voila!—you have a realist moving photographic image. The fact that the image is produced by a machine has been seen by many critics and theorists to be a key to the supposed realism of photography and the movies and to mark the chief differentiating factor between photography and painting. In the popular mind, moving pictures became associated with realism, authenticity, and reliability.

The supposed ties between movies and reality, however, caused many people to be suspicious of the capacity of the medium to create art. A mere recording device, the motion-picture camera might be useful to produce documentary imitations of the visual world, but what about the creativity and human imagination that the arts call for? How could one engage in world making, in the creation of alternative realities, when one merely used a device that mechanically recorded what was in front of it? Any art in a finished film, the thought went, was already present in front of the camera, not a result of the camera itself or any creative imagination on the part of the filmmaker.

Some observers spoke of the movies as "canned theater," the idea being that movies were simply stage plays recorded in the movie medium. A few intellectuals like the Harvard University psychologist and philosopher Hugo Munsterberg had sympathy and enthusiasm for the movies but were ashamed to be seen in a movie theater (Andrew 14). Early critics writing about film were eager to demonstrate that film could be a unique and important art form, and Munsterberg in 1916 produced the first important book of film theory, *The Film: A Psychological Study*. In that book, he wrote of a new narrative medium coming into its own, something more than the mere filming of preexistent stage plays.

Early film theory is often divided into the "formalist" and "realist" positions, with the formalists writing earlier in film history than the realist theorists, but we can also speak of a third way, the "revelationist" position, as will be discussed shortly. The formalists were interested in carving out a unique niche for the movies as a serious and distinct art form. Thus, they needed to demonstrate that movies deserved a place among the established art forms and that movies were more than the mere recording or slavish imitation of reality. Rudolph Arnheim, a central representative of that tradition, held that movies must depart from the mere imitation of reality or duplication of normal perception, because only that would make expression possible. The creative, imaginative expression of the artist would occur only when filmmakers departed from the duplication of reality. Thus, Arnheim favored the silent film because its very limitations as a recording medium (lack of sound and color) enabled it to be expressive. For Arnheim, each technological development that brought the movies closer to the recording of quotidian reality also moved the medium further from art and imaginative expression. Arnheim bemoaned the coming of color and sound, seeing these developments as catering to the masses who demanded ever-increasing realism and who cared little for artistic expression (Arnheim; Andrew 27–41; Carroll, *Philosophical* 17–91).

Arnheim failed to grasp an essential characteristic of the technologies that make movies possible. Although the coming of sound and color to the medium may increase the sense of realism afforded by movies in some regards (to be explored shortly), they also enlarged and diversified the expressive possibilities available to filmmakers. The use of various color film stocks, for example, may have allowed the world of a film to look more like the colorful visual world we are used to. Yet color film stocks can also be used creatively. In Victor Fleming's *The Wizard of Oz* (1939), for example, the filmmakers used both black-and-white and rich Technicolor film stocks to present a stark contrast between the mundane but comforting world of Kansas (sepia-toned black and white) and the fantastical Oz, featuring (in Technicolor) a yellow brick road, colorfully clad Munchkins, and an Emerald City with a pretentious but ultimately kind-hearted wizard. In Spike Lee's vibrant *Do the Right Thing* (1988), the "corner men" (Paul Benjamin, Frankie Faison, and Robin Harris) sit on old kitchen chairs in the neighborhood of Bedford-Stuyvesant and comment on everything going on around them. They are positioned in front of a bright-red, nearly featureless flat wall, the color of which pops out and creates a space for them that seems to be outside the film's fictional world. Michelangelo Antonioni takes the decaying industrial landscapes of *Red Desert* (1964) and makes images that are reminiscent of modernist paintings by employing large blocks of color and intriguing color combinations.

In the predigital age, filmmakers often manipulated color not only through the choice of film stock but also through exposure, settings, costume, makeup, gels, and lighting. Think of the green face of the Wicked Witch of the West in *The Wizard of Oz*, for example, or the complementary color scheme (red and green) used in Alfred Hitchcock's *Vertigo* (1958). Filmmakers working in the digital age have even greater technical and creative resources at their disposal. Joel and Ethan Coen's *O Brother Where Art Thou?* (2000) was one of the first productions for which digital color grading became central to its aesthetic, such grading having been used to transform the lush greens of the South in the summer into a muted palette consisting of various sepia tones and suggestive of the look of an old postcard. Today digital color grading (in conjunction with traditional analog techniques) allows for numerous creative uses of color, from the monochromatic palette of Zhang Yimou's *Hero* (2002), in which each scene features a dominant color scheme, to the pastel aesthetic of Wes Anderson's *Grand Budapest Hotel* (2014) to triadic color schemes and those experimenting with various gradations of lightness and saturation. Another expressive color technique is the selective saturation effect, where everything is in black and white (or some monochromatic variation) except for a "focal object" that gets a vivid color. Nearly all of Steven Spielberg's *Schindler's List* (1993) is photographed in black and white, but in the midst of this monochromatic world, Oscar Schindler (Liam Neeson) sees a little girl in a red coat that awakens him to the evils of the Holocaust and symbolizes the shedding of blood. None of these uses of color is wholly naturalistic (though they sometimes seem so to the viewer); all are the creative expression of the filmmakers.

Even naturalistic uses of the medium can function as creative expression. Movies are a dynamic and eclectic medium, capable of expressing ideas and impressions through numerous channels simultaneously. Thus, a particular shot may feature naturalistic color, for example, and remain an expression of the filmmakers due to the way that the shot is edited into the scene, uses sound, features expressive costumes or sets, or contains meaningful dialogue. One common technique of horror films is to combine naturalistic and nonnaturalistic elements. For example, characters may be camping out in a forest, with the visual elements of the scene presented naturalistically. They begin to hear increasingly bizarre, unidentifiable sounds emanating from the darkness, gradually disclosing a frightening world that the characters had never envisioned. The monster itself in a horror film is often some kind of impossible being. Films need to create a *sense* of reality that we call verisimilitude. But verisimilitude, as we shall see, allows for all kinds of fantastical, expressive, and imaginative elements. Arnheim thought that the popular imagination and new representational technologies would demand ever-increasing realism that would stifle creative expression. The fact that today the most popular movie genres are animated fantasy, science fiction, and superhero movies makes these fears seem quite misplaced. The realism of the movies does not necessarily overshadow creative expression and can even be put to the service of expression and fantasy.

THE REALISTS AND THE REVELATIONISTS

Opposed to the formalists were the realists. Realists believed that what is special and important about movies is their relationship to the real world. Siegfried Kracauer, who has often been identified as a realist, believed that film was essentially a photographic medium. He writes that film "is an extension of photography and therefore shares with this medium a marked affinity for the visible world around us. Films come into their own when they record and reveal physical reality" (xlix). From this comes the special power of the medium and its capacity to powerfully move viewers and teach them something. For Kracauer, realist theory had an ethical dimension. He believed that movies had the capacity to reconnect people with the physical reality around them and to deepen their relation to their native habitat, the Earth (li).

André Bazin is by far the most influential realist theorist. For Bazin as for Kracauer, the realism of the movie medium begins with its connection with photography. In "The Ontology of the Photographic Image" (in *What Is Cinema*, vol. 1), Bazin likens a photograph to a fingerprint, footprint, the shadow cast by a sundial, or an embalmed body. All register a trace of the reality that they signify. Like footprints and fossils, the photograph is related by causality to its referent (what it stands for or represents), because it is created by a mechanical device, the camera, which eliminates at least some aspects of human subjectivity (12). As Bazin writes, the "objective nature of photography confers on it a quality of credibility absent from all other picture-making" (13). This is why photographs can be used in a court of law in ways that verbal testimony or paintings are not.

Why is this important? For Bazin, this meant that the movies and photography became the ultimate realist media. This is both an ontological and a psychological claim; the mechanical nature of moving-image photography granted the movies the power to connect viewers with nature in a psychologically powerful way. Bazin even went so far as to claim that the invention of photography allowed painting to become more expressive and abstract, since painting was freed from its previous "obsession" with re-creating the world through realist representation.

For Bazin, this supposed realism that grounds the movies means that filmmakers ought to respect reality by using techniques and styles that put viewers into a relationship with the movie that is somewhat like their relationship to the outside world. Thus, Bazin favored the long-take aesthetic, consisting of durationally long shots with camera movement, over the montage style of the Soviets or the classical cutting of Hollywood. For Bazin, the elegant camera movements and composition-in-depth of directors like Orson Welles, Jean Renoir, and William Wyler constituted a mature style of filmmaking that respected the viewer's capacity to explore the reality represented in the shot. Bazin writes in "The Evolution of the Language of Cinema" that depth of focus "brings the spectator into a relation with the image closer to that which he enjoys with reality" and requires "a more active mental attitude on the part of the spectator" (*What Is Cinema?*, vol. 1, 35–36). Deep-focus composition can also preserve "ambiguity of expression," he writes, whereas the montage style "presupposes . . . the unity of meaning of the dramatic event" (36).

At the same time, Bazin also favored narrative techniques that incorporated indirection, ambiguity, and ellipsis, arguing that such realist storytelling managed to respect the ambiguity of reality and allowed the viewer a certain amount of freedom of interpretation and filling in of narrative gaps. Bazin wrote glowingly of Italian neorealism, a film movement that emerged after World War II that used actual locations and a mixture of professional and unprofessional actors. In many neorealist films, Bazin writes, a "complex train of action is reduced to three or four brief fragments, in themselves already elliptical enough in comparison with the reality they are unfolding." In making sense of these fragments, Bazin claims, the "mind has to leap from one event to the other as one leaps from stone to stone in crossing a river" (*What Is Cinema?*, vol. 2, 35). Making sense of a realist film is much like making sense of the world around us. We need to be active and sort through ambiguous information, make hypotheses about missing events, and so on.

Aside from the formalists and realists, Malcolm Turvey has identified what he calls the "revelationist" tradition, an approach to the medium that seems to draw from elements of both formalist and realist theory in its approach to how film ought to be conceptualized vis-à-vis reality ("Balázs"; *Doubting*). For Turvey, theorists such as Jean Epstein, Dziga Vertov, Bela Balázs, and Siegfried Kracauer should be seen as neither formalists (or "modernists," as he terms it) nor realists. Like the realists, the revelationists take the capacity of the motion-picture medium to reproduce reality to be a valuable one. Unlike Bazin, however, the revelationists do not believe that human vision can be trusted. As Turvey notes, the revelationists "view those stylistic techniques that depart from everyday sight as most likely to reveal reality as it really is" ("Balázs" 88). Bela Balázs insisted that human beings are very bad at noticing details and that for this reason film techniques like the close-up take on a special importance in filmmaking. Remember that for Bazin, close-ups break up reality, and for that reason he favored the long take, which tended to be also a more panoramic sort of long shot. As Balázs puts it, "a good film with its close-ups reveals the most hidden parts in our polyphonous life, and teaches us to see the intricate visual details of life" (qtd. in "Balázs" 85). The revelationist tradition thus effected a kind of compromise between realist and formalist film theories.

FORMS OF REALISM

A next step would be to define our terms. What is realism, and what are the various sorts of realism in movies? Verisimilitude, as introduced earlier, is the *subjective impres-*

sion that a movie, scene, setting, character, or story is real or believable. To most moviemakers, verisimilitude is absolutely vital, as it is considered to be a precondition for the spectator's absorption into and enjoyment of the movie. The characters must act in ways that seem real; the perception of bad acting will often cause disdain for the movie and increase the psychological distance of the spectator. The world of the movie need not be just like ours. It can have flying cars, spiders the size of houses, or even characters with superpowers. In *Black Panther* (2018), we are asked to believe in a fictional world in which the nation of Wakanda is the most technologically sophisticated nation on Earth but where (in a decidedly less sophisticated fashion) the succession of political rulers is determined not by voting or political intrigue but by ritual combat. But believe it we do. The world created need not be familiar to our own world in every way. But it must seem consistent and believable while we watch.

Movies are also especially prone to what can be called "dating," whereby their dialogue or special effects seem outdated and "cheesy." Most everything about filmmaking is in a constant state of change, as technologies, stylistic techniques, and story conventions are in continuous flux. Students sometimes have trouble enjoying "old" movies because the black-and-white film stock, acting styles, special effects, or idiomatic speech of the past seem naïve or clumsy. For these students, old films may lack verisimilitude. We often judge the products of the past by the conventions of the present, failing to understand that these contemporary "realist" conventions that go unnoticed today may strike future audiences as quaint or even laughable.

"Ontological realism" is completely different from verisimilitude, despite many critics seeming to blur the two terms, as Bazin arguably seems to do. Whereas verisimilitude describes a perception of "realness," ontological realism describes an *actual* relationship between a movie and the real world. Ontology, a branch of philosophy, is the study of the nature of being. A movie that is ontologically realistic, then, is *like* or *conforms with* the reality it represents in one or more respects. Some people claim that the opening of Steven Spielberg's *Saving Private Ryan* (1998) captures the sights and sounds of violent battle like no other film before it. The film begins with a twenty-seven-minute scene that shows the assault by the Americans on Omaha Beach during the Allied invasion of Normandy in World War II. The *Los Angeles Times* critic Kenneth Turan called it a "powerful and impressive milestone in the realistic depiction of combat." It is controversial whether such talk of realism as a statement of the ontological status of a movie is legitimate. Relativists deny that reality itself has fixed ontological status; if reality lacked any fixed characteristics, then of course one film would be as ontologically unreal (or real) as another. The "critical realist" perspective, on the other hand, holds that there is a real world and that as long as the term "realism" is carefully used, ascribing levels of realism to a film or scene may be legitimate. Some films just do provide a more accurate sense of their subject matter than others. Stanley Kubrick's *2001: A Space Odyssey* (1968), with its lonely silences, may give us a much more realistic sense of what being in space might sound like than does George Lucas's *Star Wars* (1977), which makes space sound a lot like sound within the atmosphere of the Earth. (After all, sounds cannot be produced or heard without a medium such as air or water.) This is not to belittle *Star Wars*. It should be noted that realism or its lack, when taken in its ontological sense, is neutral with regard to the aesthetic excellence of a movie. Realism is not *necessarily* an aesthetically good thing.

When discussing ontological realism, one distinction that will be useful is between objective and subjective realism. A movie that is objectively realistic provides a plausibly accurate rendition of some aspect of the real world. A film that is subjectively realistic provides a plausible rendition of the way in which a particular character *experiences* that world. For an example of objective realism, consider Debra Granik's *Winter's Bone* (2010), based on the novel of the same name by Daniel Woodrell. In this film, Jennifer Lawrence stars as Ree Dolly, a teenaged girl living with her family in the rural Ozarks of Missouri. With her mother mentally ill and her father missing (and possibly dead), she is forced to care for her younger sister and brother through very hard times. Set against a backdrop of the underworld of drug manufacturing and family secrets, the film explores the nature of close and distant family ties, poverty, and resilience and provides an illuminating portrait of its subjects and their environment.

Granik's commitment to realism is everywhere apparent, and she says that she wanted to "show the lives of ordinary citizens who have to live with very limited material resources" (Jenkins). The movie's actual locations and use of local extras (in some cases as major characters) create a strong sense of place. Ree Dolly's home is the actual home of a local resident, and one of Ree's siblings is played by this resident's then-six-year-old granddaughter. Local musicians appear in the movie playing traditional music characteristic of the area, and the movie employs other actual locations, for example, a burned-out building that was actually a meth lab (Ulaby). None of this guarantees authenticity, and any estimation of what the film gets right and wrong would be subject to further research. (It has been said, for example, that the film fails to show the proper means of butchering a squirrel.) Nevertheless, one could make the case that *Winter's Bone* provides an objectively realistic sense of a particular place and time.

Subjective realism, rather than providing an accurate sense of a place or event from the outside in, might be said to provide a representation of someone's experience from the inside out. Danny Boyle's *Trainspotting* (1996), for example, presents the experience of both a high from heroin and the "junkie limbo" of getting off it expressively through the use of distorted and wide-angle lenses, camera movement, impossible perspectives (a baby crawling across the ceiling, for example), hallucinations, distorted sound effects, and underscoring. All of this, arguably, is an authentic expression of the *kind* of feelings and experiences one may have when using heroin or detoxing. Of course, one does not typically hear underscoring during detox (although one can listen to music), yet such music contributes to the overall mood of the scenes, which could be argued to be fitting. From an objective perspective, the scenes are surrealistic. From the junkie's perspective, however, they may be an accurate rendering of the subjective experience of using and getting off heroin.

So far we have discussed verisimilitude and two types of ontological realism: objective and subjective realism. What makes all discussions of realism problematic is that reality is complex and multifaceted. The distinction between objective and subjective realism captures the sense that there is a distinction between the objective world and a character's individual experience of that world, though both are ultimately aspects of the same world. Further distinctions can be made, however. As Timothy Corrigan and Patricia White note, realism is one "of the most common, complicated, and elusive yardsticks for the cinema" (70).

We can speak of psychological realism (plausibility of character traits and the interactions of characters), scenic realism (the physical and historical accuracy of sets and costumes), narrative realism (plausible developments and progressions in the story), and perceptual realism (the replication of the way the world looks and/or sounds to an observer). Certainly we can make legitimate judgments about realism in some cases, and we in fact do that all the time. When we claim that a movie is too idealized or misrepresents an ethnic group or race of people or has laughable and unbelievable dialogue, these are all judgments of realism. Yet when making such judgments, it is often easy to overlook the fact that what seems "real" to us may seem artificial to others. For this reason, many critics prefer to think of realism as verisimilitude—a *seeming* to be real, rather than a description of an ontological relationship between a film and reality.

If all of this were not enough to demonstrate that *realism* is a term fraught with ambiguity, we should also note that "realism" is often used to designate movies with social concerns or movies that use certain kinds of stylistic or formal techniques. As a genre, realist movies are thought to have a social purpose; they represent the poor, the old, and the dispossessed, as we saw in the case of *Winter's Bone*. Realist movies are often social-problem films. Instead of rags-to-riches stories or tales of superheroes, aliens, or ghosts, a realist film such as Vittorio De Sica's *Bicycle Thieves* (*Ladri di biciclette*, 1948) shows the travails of a working-class man and his family, as the man desperately searches for his stolen bicycle, which is essential for his continued employment and ability to provide for his family. Realism in this sense focuses squarely on society and its problems.

Realism is also sometimes characterized by techniques associated with the observational documentary: the shaky camera, rapid zooms in and out, swish pans, violations of editing continuity, and characters glancing at and acknowledging the camera. Such stylistic realism is a feature of many feature films but has also come to characterize a whole genre of television comedies (Thompson). Among these are *The Office* (2005–13), *Arrested Development* (2003–), *Parks and Recreation* (2009–15), and *Modern Family* (2009–). Although these programs are entirely fictional, their documentary-like style provides them a sense of authenticity and verisimilitude. We also saw earlier in Bazin's discussion of Italian neorealism that certain styles of narrative are often associated with realism. Bazin thought that ellipses in storytelling were ontologically realistic. To give another example, the Hollywood happy ending is often thought to be ontologically unrealistic, serving to cater to the wish-fulfilling fantasies of popular audiences, while the mixed, ambiguous, and open ending is widely thought to be more realistic (MacDowell 98–132).

THREE HYPOTHESES ABOUT THE MOVIE MEDIUM

Now let us return to André Bazin's realism in order to introduce three hypotheses about the movie medium in relation to realism. It would be unfair to characterize Bazin as a "naïve realist," that is, as one who assumes that films are simple reflections of the real world and who fails to understand the ineluctable creativity and imagination to go into the making of any film. Bazin realized that the simple imitation or recording of reality is not and cannot be descriptive of any work of art or art form. "The faithful reproduction of reality," he writes, "is not art" (*What Is Cinema?*, vol. 2, 64). But Bazin wrote of realism without carefully distinguishing between its many varieties: verisimilitude, ontological realism, and realism as a socially concerned orientation. Moreover, Bazin sometimes struggled to reconcile the creative process essential to art with the photographic realism he held to underlie the movie medium.

Bazin claimed, for example, that the "neorealist film has a meaning, but it is *a posteriori* . . . whereas in the classical artistic composition the meaning is established *a priori*" (*What Is Cinema?*, vol. 2, 99) or, in other words, before the film is made. This would seem to characterize the making of an Italian neorealist film as one of discovery. Yet Bazin praises Italian neorealist film for its "fundamental humanism" and sees this as the films' "chief merit" (21). It would be odd to believe that the neorealist filmmakers, film after film, discovered their humanist perspective only after the fact. One would think that Vittorio De Sica, Roberto Rossellini, and other neorealist filmmakers chose their topics and methods in large part due to their prior humanist convictions. In response to Bazin's vagueness about the nature of realism, his theory has been subject to numerous contradictory interpretations (Carroll, *Philosophical*; Henderson 32–47; Morgan).

In response to these issues, we can make three observations that we will consider as hypotheses. The first is that all films, realist or not, are dependent on the expressive "vision" and rhetorical intentions of the filmmaker(s); all films create "worlds"; all films are products of the human imagination. Thus, no film is a mere recording of the world out there. Not even documentaries can be considered to be mere imitations or recordings, as I argue in chapter 5. As V. F. Perkins writes, movies offer two tendencies. First, movies have the power to "'possess' the real world by capturing its appearance" (60). By this, Perkins is referring to perceptual realism and verisimilitude. On the other hand, however, movies abide by traditional aesthetic concerns and present an "ideal image" that is "ordered by the film-maker's will and imagination" (60).

The second hypothesis is that discussions of realism in its various forms can still be useful, as long as such discussions take into account the complexity of "realism" and its various meanings. For example, the claim that a scene has verisimilitude must be distinguished from the claim that a scene is objectively realistic. Even animated fantasies can have verisimilitude in the sense that the created world has consistent rules or laws and in the sense that the characters might interact with each other in ways that seem psychologically plausible.

To make the claim that a realist film such as *Winter's Bone* is objectively realistic raises various complications. Claims of objective realism seem to demand some objective testimony or evidence. Moreover, it is difficult to make the claim that certain movie styles or techniques are more realist than others. The happy ending, for example, is widely credited with being unreal (MacDowell 98–132).

But are there no happy endings in life? Do things never go well for us? Sometimes they do, fortunately. People sometimes get to marry the person of their dreams. Bad guys are caught, lost dogs find their way home, and puppies are sometimes rescued after falling into wells. A screen story that ends happily is not *necessarily* unrealistic. As James MacDowell notes, happy endings may certainly reflect naïve wish fulfillment, excessive conventionality, or the problems associated with narrative closure generally (closure tends to make an untidy world seem tidy), yet a partly happy ending that suggests an inevitably uncertain future, such as the ending of *Eternal Sunshine of the Spotless Mind* (2004), may escape the charge of "unreality" (130–31). And as some romantic comedies imply, a good romantic partnership can sometimes last a lifetime.

The trouble with banishing all talk of objective realism is that it would then be difficult to discuss the way that screen stories can sometimes be either illuminating or misleading. We need to hold out the possibility that *Winter's Bone* can give us a sense of what it might be like to live in poverty in the rural Ozarks of Missouri or that *Trainspotting* may provide something of the phenomenology of a heroin-induced drug trip or that *2001: A Space Odyssey* may provide a sense of what space travel might be like and *Star Wars* not so much. Even fictional fantasies incorporate assumptions about what the world is like and of what people are like. If we cannot discuss ontological realism, it becomes very difficult to think about the relationship of stories to the real world. Difficult as these discussions are, they are vital to the function of stories in human life and to an ethics of screen stories.

Third and most important, we need to recognize that film is not, in its essence, a photographic medium. This may seem a bold and counterintuitive statement, so it needs some unpacking. Both Bazin and Kracauer saw film as essentially photographic, which led them to construct theories that characterized the movies as a medium that needed to "respect," record, and/or reveal reality. But this characterization downplayed or ignored animated and avant-garde films. Winsor McKay showed us the animated Gertie in *Gertie the Dinosaur* as early as 1914, and Georges Méliès was experimenting with stop-motion animation before that. From the beginning, it was possible to make films that were not photographic, either wholly or in part. And today, with the rise of digital image technologies, the ease with which artists can use software to alter or even wholly construct seemingly realistic images throws into question claims that the movies depend fundamentally on cameras.

For this reason, it is more accurate to say film is a *composite* medium. Stephen Prince argues that the "photographic biasing and the live action biasing that have existed in generations of thought and theory about the movies have tended to deflect attention from the extent to which cinema is a composted collage of different ingredients" (23). Among these ingredients are sometimes moving photographic images but also animated images, digitally altered or enhanced images, graphics and titles, and abstract, nonrepresentational shapes. And the images themselves are edited into a sequence, accompanied by a soundtrack, and in the case of a fiction film have been designed and planned based on a screenplay. The soundtrack, editing, and screenplay have as much claim to the essence of film as the cinematography does—that is, none. Film is a composite medium in which worlds are constructed through the combination of discrete elements.

What does this have to do with realism in film? Most importantly, it undermines any claim that film is essentially rooted in photographic realism. Photographic realism is still important, of course. But it cannot be said to be characteristic of film *as a medium*. Seeing film as a composite medium helps us to understand that films are rhetorical, imaginative, creative constructs that *may* in some cases incorporate realist moving photographic images.

REALISM AND ETHICS

One last important topic needs to be mentioned: the relationship between verisimilitude and ideology. An important strain of film theory, what we can call "estrangement theory," distrusts mainstream movies for ideological reasons having to do with realism. Earlier we examined the distinction between verisimilitude and ontological realism. A movie that has verisimilitude has the quality of seeming to be realistic in some regard, while a movie that is ontologically realistic *actually is* accurate, insightful, and/or realistic in some regard. Estrangement theorists believe that audiences of mainstream narrative films and media are likely to mistake verisimilitude for ontological realism and that this makes mainstream screen stories, which encourage an immersive effect, ideologically problematic. What seems to be real may be completely false but is presented compellingly in a way that causes the spectator to take it as truth. What is artificial is presented as natural. What is rhetorically dubious is presented as realistic.

The distrust of the effects of narrative art is deep and wide and has a long history (Plantinga, *Screen* 14–21). In film and media theory, it manifests itself in the critical theory of Theodor Adorno and Max Horkheimer, neo-Brechtian film theory, and the apparatus theory rooted in Lacanian psychoanalysis and Althusserian Marxist critique (Plantinga, *Screen* 99–107). Stories on screens have a power and allure that can influence cultures and individuals. They make a case or, in other words, suggest and favor attitudes, perspectives, and appropriate responses based on what is in the story and how it is presented. Screen stories can cause powerful emotions, immerse the spectator, and use verisimilitude to convince audiences that their assumptions are "natural" or "obvious." Such is the rhetorical potential of this powerful art form.

These warnings are well taken but one-sided. Estrangement theorists tend to focus on the ways in which films—and especially mainstream films—are misleading, distorted, or ideological spurious. And indeed, many of them are. But certainly some films are not or, at least, are not wholly so. An ethics of realism should also recognize that screen stories have the capacity to provide genuine insight into a situation or event, to elicit empathy by showing us what it might be like to be someone wholly different from ourselves, or even to increase the viewer's moral sophistication by presenting a protagonist's artful solutions to complex ethical problems (Plantinga, *Screen*; Sinnerbrink; Stadler). Thus, realism is potentially problematic from an ethical perspective. But it also has the potential to teach and inspire. Whether a film does one or the other (or both) must be determined on a case-by-case basis.

2

FANTASY AND REALITY

In chapter 1, we saw that although realism is thought to be central to the movie medium, even the most realist of movies are expressive, rhetorical constructs. An over-emphasis on realism in the cinema (and especially on its photographic nature) threatens to overshadow the creative aspects of movie art and the many ways in which screen stories diverge from the world as we experience it. If moving images are a realist medium, then what explains the popularity of fantasies, science fiction, and super-hero films? Of the fifty top-grossing films internationally, all but three fit squarely into one of these genres or else mix them together. And fantasies (animated and/or live action) make up more than one half of the top-grossing films internationally. One of the top-grossing films of all time is James Cameron's *Avatar* (2009), set on the planet Pandora and featuring interactions between humans and the Na'vi, an alien race of bluish ten-foot-tall aliens with large yellow eyes and sweeping tails. And tremendously popular superhero films give us fantastical beings who can spin webs like spiders, swing like trapeze artists, stop rushing locomotives in their tracks, or leap tall buildings in a single bound.

The early French filmmaker Georges Méliès tilted the medium toward fantasy beginning well over a century ago. His films provided us with devils, fairies, nymphs, aliens, sea creatures, and other imaginary beings that populate fantastical worlds. Throughout film history, fantasy and science fiction have been a staple of motion pictures. *The Wizard of Oz* (1939), *Star Wars* (1977), and Richard Donner's *Superman* (1978) all are beloved classics. Yet with the rise of digital special effects, these genres, together with the superhero film, have begun to absolutely dominate worldwide box office. Digital effects can convincingly represent what we normally believe to be impossible. Digital effects brought us the "liquid effect," shape shifting, and morphing of the T-1000 (Robert Patrick) in James Cameron's *Terminator 2: Judgment Day* (1991). Digital effects brought us the dinosaurs of Steven Spielberg's *Jurassic Park* (1993) and the Winklevoss identical twins (both played by Armie Hammer) in David Fincher's *The Social Network* (2010). Through the use of green screens before which real actors fight, run, and otherwise cavort, digital effects allow filmmakers to create composites of fantastical digital mattes with live-action cinematography. Motion capture allows film-makers to record an actor's facial expressions and move-ments, then map those onto digital creatures such as Gollum (Andy Serkis) in Peter Jackson's *The Lord of the Rings: The Fellowship of the Ring* (2001), the ape Caesar (Andy Serkis) in Matt Reeves's *War for the Planet of the Apes* (2017), or the dragon Smaug (Benedict Cumber-batch) in Peter Jackson's *The Hobbit: The Desolation of Smaug* (2013). Filmmakers have long been able to manip-ulate time through fast and slow motion, but recent tech-niques such as "bullet time" make use of dozens of still cameras to temporally and spatially detach what is shown from the camera (and the viewer). Not only can events be slowed down significantly more than in traditional slow motion, but the camera's (and viewer's) perspective can change in real time as this occurs. All this seems to put the fiction into a different dimension altogether. Thus, in *The Matrix* (1999), Neo (Keanu Reaves) can seemingly sus-pend his body above the ground while dodging bullets, and Trinity (Carrie-Anne Moss) can engage in a gunfight while trotting horizontally across vertical walls.

One could legitimately conclude that the movie medium is best at telling fantastical stories that are wholly different from the world we inhabit and that these films provide nothing but an escape from our mundane lives, pleasurable wish fulfillment for patrons in need of comfort and excitement. Any such claim, however, would be simplistic and misleading. Fantasies on the screen remain firmly rooted in quotidian reality, and their popularity depends in part on their ability to elicit responses in audiences that are rooted in their everyday lives. Superheroes, for example, are still recognizably human. They have bodies; they think, plan, feel, and respond; they develop social bonds with others and can become lonely; they can be hurt both physically and psychologically. And the Na'vi—the alien race from another world—speak, think, and behave in ways remarkably similar to the human beings who invade their planet.

Stephen Prince, in his book about digital visual effects, writes of "cheating physics," which occurs when CGI characters disobey certain physical laws and the CGI looks "cheesy" and unconvincing (74–104). This phenomenon is both fascinating and mysterious. Audiences easily accept the capacity of Superman to fly through the air and for Wonder Woman to trace bullets as they speed toward her and then use her lightning-quick reflexes and magical wrist guards to shield herself from them. Nonetheless, when Spiderman swings from skyscraper to skyscraper, or when the Incredible Hulk jumps up fifty feet and then lands with a heavy thud, we expect that the actions will be rendered in such a way that they seem plausible. We expect that Spiderman will swing in such a way that the laws of momentum will be respected and that the Hulk will land with an appropriate thud that shakes the firmament as though a heavy weight had dropped to the ground. We welcome and accept certain divergences from the world as we experience it, but in other respects, we demand that fantastical representations correspond with that world. Verisimilitude can be a curious thing indeed.

The rich worlds of fantasy depend on a spectator to fill in the gaps. A filmmaker cannot provide every detail possible to bring to life the alternative world presented. It is the presumptions of the spectator that fully flesh out those worlds. And those presumptions derive in part from the viewer's real-world experience. If an animated mouse has a face (as does Mickey Mouse), we presume that, like the human face, it will register emotion that is a clue to inner thought and feeling. If five fantastical beings gather to discuss a plan, we presume that their conversation will in most ways follow social conventions for group planning. If we meet the daughter of a God (as in *Wonder Woman*), we presume that since she is young, beautiful, and unattached, she will be romantically interested in a handsome young man she rescues from a plane crash. From whence come these assumptions? As David Bordwell writes, some of them come from our experience with other films, media, and the arts. This is probably true of our expectation that Wonder Woman will find romance. But the bulk of them "must derive from automatic mechanisms we use to make sense of the physical world we live in. There is just too much information onscreen that would call for too much dedicated processing otherwise" (*Poetics* 111). We bring our real-world perceptual, cognitive, and social skills to bear on our experience of fictional world. Bordwell notes (citing Marie-Laure Ryan) that we tend to make sense of story worlds according to the "Principal of Minimal Departure" (112). We presume that everything about these worlds corresponds to our everyday reality, unless the text specifies otherwise. And the filmmakers, of course, know this.

Even the most fantastical stories are rooted in the spectator's experience of the everyday physical world. This is what this chapter will demonstrate, using as examples the superhero film *Wonder Woman* (2017), the science-fiction fantasy *Guardians of the Galaxy* (2014), and Disney Studio's depictions of Mickey Mouse. The correspondences between fantasy and reality are numerous, but here we will highlight three of the most important: the depiction of the face in animation, the reliance on intuitive psychology and social schemas for characterization, and connections to common moral concerns and cultural memes.

ANIMATED FACES AND MICKEY MOUSE

Cartoons and animation offer us imaginary universes that in some ways are much different from our own world. Yet it is remarkable the degree to which even animation relies for its power on psychological processes that viewers use to make sense of the everyday world. In the West, nearly everyone is familiar with Mickey Mouse, the famous cartoon character dreamed up by the animators Walt Disney and Ub Iwerks for Disney Studios in the 1920s. A brief history of changes in the way that Mickey Mouse was (and is) drawn will serve to demonstrate the important relationship between the visual appearance of animated characters and audience responses that are both biologically and culturally rooted. These responses are firmly dependent on the spectator's experience of and responses to faces—both human and animal.

The film historian and cultural critic Robert Sklar, in his influential *Movie-Made America: A Cultural History of American Movies*, notes that Frank Capra, Walt Disney, and other successful filmmakers of the 1930s became acutely aware of the increasing cultural power of movies and of their role as mythmakers. In the case of Disney, one can see this in the evolution of the Mickey Mouse cartoons between 1928 and 1933. One of the first of these cartoons was *Steamboat Willie* (1928), which, as Sklar writes, exhibited "bold inventiveness with integrated visual and sound effects [that] gave animated shorts a popularity and aesthetic significance they had never had before" (199). Sklar notes that during these years, the Disney animators became more sophisticated and their animation more polished. Along with this, however, came a change to Mickey Mouse himself. As the Disney cartoons became moral tales, Mickey transformed from a vulgar mischief maker free "from the burdens of time and responsibility" to a "respectable, bland, gentle, responsible, moral" bore (200). In *Steamboat Willie*, Mickey makes Bronx cheers at his rival Pete, silences a parrot by throwing a wooden bucket over him, plays a cow's teeth as though they were a xylophone, and stretches ducks' necks to make rhythmic quacking sounds. This sort of irresponsible fun disappeared as Mickey became a national figure.

Sklar also notes changes in Mickey's appearance, which relate more directly to the fantasy-reality interface that is the subject of this chapter. The early Mickey was very much a rodent, his limbs thinner and features smaller than the increasingly anthropomorphic Mickey of later years. In the early cartoons, Mickey was likely to be barefoot and bare-handed, while the later Mickey donned shoes and white four-fingered gloves. Mickey's increasing anthropomorphism corresponded with a move toward conventionality in the animation itself. Whereas the early Disney cartoons were inventive and anarchic, the new, "socially responsible" Disney was strictly conformist. As Sklar writes, "The borders to fantasy are closed now. The time has come to lay aside one's own imagination, and together all shall dream Walt Disney's dreams" (205).

The underpinnings of Mickey's "great change" are explained differently in an essay by the famous biologist Steven Jay Gould, entitled "A Biological Homage to Mickey Mouse." Like Sklar, Gould notices changes in the appearance of Mickey Mouse from the late 1920s through the 1950s. Gould calls it a "progressive juvenilization" (263). Over the years, Mickey's face changes substantially. We see a gradual increase in the size of his eyes and head in relation to the rest of his body; his ears move back; his legs and arms thicken and grow pudgy; and his snout becomes shorter. Not only is Mickey anthropomorphized, as Sklar notices, but he is increasingly given childlike facial and body features. Whereas Sklar attributes these changes to Disney's self-conscious awareness of his role as cultural mythmaker, Gould attributes them to an "unconscious" realization among Disney animators of audience reactions to "cuteness" (267).

Why cuteness? Human children, compared to adults, have proportionally larger eyes, a smaller jaw, a massive cranium, and short, pudgy arms and legs. Gould cites

Konrad Lorenz's claim that the facial and body features of children trigger affection and tendencies toward nurturing in adults (265). Adults respond to this cuteness factor not only in infant humans but also in infant animals that feature these facial characteristics. (Two-dimensional representations of animals can trigger similar responses, as the Bambi cartoons illustrate.) Lorenz notes that adult animals with these facial features, such as squirrels, rabbits, and robins, also elicit warm responses in humans, whereas long-snouted, small-eyed animals do not. He notes that typically we regard the camel as aloof and unfriendly because it seems to mimic the "gesture of haughty rejection" (qtd. in Gould 267) common to many cultures. Humans even respond in similar fashion to inanimate objects that mimic human facial features and that trigger these basic warmth and nurture responses. In any case, Gould claims that the evolution of Mickey's appearance "reflects the unconscious discovery of this biological principle by Disney and his artists" (267), who presumably wanted to make Mickey more likeable and popular and did this by emphasizing juvenile facial and body features and thus emphasizing his cuteness.

By contrast, notice the facial and body features of Mortimer Mouse, who appears in the 1936 short *Mickey's Rival*, directed by Wilfred Jackson. Mortimer, a narcissistic dandy who drives a yellow sports car, vies with

Mickey for the attentions of Minnie Mouse. Audiences are not meant to have warm feelings toward Mortimer. In this regard, the way he is drawn is very interesting. As Gould notes, Mortimer is much more adult-like, taller and thinner. His head is also more mature: "The thoroughly disreputable Mortimer has a head only 29 percent of his body length, to Mickey's 45, and a snout 80 percent of his head length, compared to Mickey's 49" (268). We might also note that Mortimer looks more like a rat than a mouse and that mice are closer to having juvenile facial features than beady-eyed rats are.

Gould writes of the "unconscious discovery" of the biological principle of cuteness in the evolution of Mickey onscreen. In a sense, we can conceive of filmmaking as a laboratory of film structure and style. A technique is tried and judged to fail or succeed according to the intuitive sense of the animators and the perceived success of the technique with the broader audience. Those techniques and structures that fail are discarded. Those that succeed become part of the filmmaking canon. Elsewhere I call this the "filmmaker-audience loop" (Plantinga, "Folk").

The techniques used not only in animation but also in all the registers of movie communication and expression must have an interface with human psychology; they must conform to the human embodied mind to have their power. But they are not for that reason natural or transparent. They are not used merely to elicit natural human responses or mental activities. Rather, as taken up by filmmakers, such techniques and structures are manipulated such that they exaggerate, focus, counter, or otherwise alter human response. The point is that even animated fantasies must conform to the requirements of their audience, to the nature of the human embodied mind. Editing, storytelling, lighting, shot composition, camera movement, and sound all must relate to the spectator's perceptual, emotive, and cognitive capacities—to the way that we respond to the everyday world around us.

They also must correspond to contemporary cultural trends, interests, and codes, as will be explored in relation to *Wonder Woman* later in this chapter. As such, films are in part conventional, and much as they draw from human perceptual, cognitive, and affective capacities, they also draw from their historical and cultural context. Both biology and culture are external realities with which fantasies must correspond and to which they in part refer.

THEORY OF MIND AND *GUARDIANS OF THE GALAXY*

This chapter takes for granted that fantasies take us outside of our quotidian existence, showing us characters and settings that are far different from our experience of everyday reality. Thus, in *Guardians of the Galaxy*, we meet a ragtag group of beings thrown together by circumstance. They decide to take a dangerously powerful "orb" from an evil villain intent on using it to destroy worlds and control the universe. Among these beings is one human, the "starlord" Peter Quill (Chris Pratt); the rest are aliens or genetic mutants of one sort or another. Gamora (Zoe Saldana) is a green-skinned female with humanoid features and superhuman fighting capacities; Rocket is a cybernetically and genetically altered raccoon (voiced by Bradley Cooper); Groot (Vin Diesel) is a tree-like humanoid with assorted skills and strengths; and the gray-and-red-skinned Drax the Destroyer (Dave Bautista) is a muscle-bound and kindhearted alien intent on revenge for the murder of his family. Like most superheroes, their physical capacities extend far beyond those of any actual human. Aside from Quill, they do not look exactly human either, though in the case of Gamora and Drax the Destroyer, the differences extend only to skin color and a few other minor traits.

Though remarkable in some ways, in the most important ways possible, all of these characters are humanlike, in that they are "persons." That is, they have a mental life—featuring intentionality, feelings, goals, and desires—that we take to be characteristic of the people around us in our social world. This is another way that fantasies remain firmly grounded in quotidian reality.

One does not have to look far to find correspondences between fantasy characters and real people. A fantasy character can diverge only so far from humanity before it ceases to have personhood, as humans conceive of it. Thus, whether the character is Daffy Duck, the Queen of Hearts, Scooby Doo, or Marge Simpson, all are recognizably characterized as persons. Thus, the Principal of Minimal Departure (described earlier) extends to our assumptions about characters in fantasy; unless specified otherwise in the text, we presume that they will behave in ways we believe people would behave.

What characterizes a person is a mental life that consists of all of those things we find to be central to our humanity—thoughts, desires, feelings, intentions, plans, goals, and the like. In our social lives, we spend much of our social time estimating just how other people employ these things. We "read" their minds. One of the central uses of narrative fiction is to consider and learn from fictional characters in relation to their presumed mental lives. As Brian Boyd writes, fiction "helps us to understand ourselves, to think—emotionally, imaginatively, reflectively—about human behavior and to step outside the immediate pressures and the automatic reactions of the moment" (208). Lisa Zunshine, in a similar fashion, argues that interaction with fictions "provides grist for the mills of our mind-reading adaptations that have evolved to deal with real people" (16).

That fantasy fiction deals with the goals, plans, and in general the interactions of characters is plainly visible in *Guardians of the Galaxy*. This film takes a somewhat ironic stance toward itself and its construction, in this case offering a scene that pokes fun at the schemas of character interaction in fiction. And here is another touchstone to everyday reality: social schemas. Schemas are a form of mental architecture on which our sense-making fundamentally depends. These schemas come in all sorts: some are specific to the conventions of screen storytelling; others have to do with the world outside; some are ambiguous or mixed. Some of these schemas are procedural in nature.

We have schemas, for example, about how a conversation ought to occur, including expectations of turn taking, listening, responding, following and developing the general topic being discussed, how and when to change topics, and what sorts of contributions to the conversation are appropriate. When someone is discussing a sad event, you do not respond with a silly "knock knock" joke. We also have schemas regarding more specific types of conversations, such as might occur, for example, when a group of persons try to formulate a plan of action for the future. Such a schema might include everything in the general conversational schema plus conventions about how to negotiate differences of opinion, come to a consensus, and then consolidate that consensus with a commitment to an agreed-on plan among the group.

One scene from *Guardians of the Galaxy* will serve to illustrate how the film relies on such schemas and the expectations they elicit from audiences. The five guardians—Quill, Gamora, Rocket, Groot, and Drax the Destroyer—are together in Yondu Odanta's spaceship, negotiating with each other and coming to a consensus about what to do next. They first criticize Rocket's previous plan to rescue Quill and Gamora:

QUILL: You want to talk about senseless. You were going to blow us up.

ROCKET: We were only going to blow you up if they didn't turn you over.

QUILL: And how in the hell were they going to turn us over when you only gave them a count of five?

ROCKET: We didn't have time to work out the minutiae of the plan. This is what we get for acting altruistically.

The scene clearly follows many of the expectations regarding conversations—turn taking, listening, responding, for example. Gamora then introduces the new plan: "What is important now is that we get the Ravager's army to help us save Zandar." The conversation continues, and the new plan develops, the scene ending when Quill gives a rousing speech that consolidates the purpose for the plan and the commitment of the five Guardians to carry it through despite the real possibility of their deaths.

The scene depicts a conversation in some ways rooted in social schemas and conversational conventions, but what makes it interesting are the ways that such schemas and conventions are humorously flouted. In fact, it is the incongruous nature of the conversation that makes it funny and even charming. The incongruities in the scene come not just from the characters occasionally failing to abide by the conventions of conversation but from a gently ironic treatment of the conventions of similar plan-making, mission-commitment scenes in hundreds of caper films.

The first incongruity is the flimsiness of the plan itself, which constitutes a kind of tongue-in-cheek comment on story conventions in similar films, relying on the savvy spectator to pick up on the humor. After the discussion of Rocket's previous ill-conceived plan to save his comrades and Gamora's insistence that they need to focus on a new goal (saving Zandar), Quill announces that he has a plan, resulting in banter that draws attention to the conventions of conversation itself:

QUILL: I have a plan.

ROCKET: You've got a plan?

QUILL: Yes.

ROCKET: First of all, you're copying me from when I said I had a plan.

QUILL: No, I'm not. People say that all the time. It's not that unique of a thing to say.

Upon further questioning, Quill admits that it is only "part" of a plan, then estimates that it is about 12 percent of a plan:

ROCKET: 12 percent? Hahahahahahahaha.

QUILL: That's a fake laugh.

ROCKET: It's real.

QUILL: Totally fake.

ROCKET: That was the most real, authentic, hysterical laugh of my entire life because that is not a plan.

GAMORA: It's barely a concept.

To participate in a conversation is to engage in mind reading, that is, to estimate the meaning of what your conversational partners say and how they respond to what you say. Thus, Quill accuses Rocket of faking laughter, and Rocket insists hyperbolically that the laugh was the most authentic of his life. Although Quill's plan is admittedly less than half-baked, he nonetheless makes the expected emotional appeal to the group, saying that life has given them a chance to "give a shit," to "not run away," and to take action against the evil Ronan. One by one, the group emotionally pledges allegiance to Quill and his plan, setting up the next act of the film.

What makes the scene effective is that it manages to abide by the conventions of conversation, plan making, and storytelling to a degree that keeps the spectator's interest, while simultaneously thwarting those conventions with divergences that become funny precisely because the audience senses that divergence. The entire scene is light and ironic, causing the spectator to search for further ironies and divergences from the norm. Part of the humor is that the group solemnly pledges its allegiance to a plan each member knows is half-baked. Additional humor comes from characters who fail to follow a basic requirement of conversation—listening—as Drax does here:

QUILL: We've already established that you destroying the ship that I'm on is not saving me.

DRAX: When did we establish that?

QUILL: Like just three seconds ago.

DRAX: I wasn't listening. I was thinking of something else.

ROCKET: She's right. You don't get an opinion.

And we have not yet mentioned Groot, the tree character whose only line is "I am Groot." Groot humorously speaks his line at the most inappropriate times. After Rocket defends his initial plan to save his comrades, Groot chimes in:

ROCKET: We didn't have time to work out the minutiae of the plan. This is what we get for acting altruistically.

GROOT: I am Groot.

ROCKET: They are ungrateful.

While the audience laughs at Groot's one-liner, they also begin to note that Rocket and perhaps other characters seem to understand that "I am Groot" can have conventional meanings depending on conversational context. When Quill reveals that he has only 12 percent of a plan and Rocket laughs, Groot responds with the usual "I am Groot," and Rocket replies, "So what, it's better than 11 percent. What the hell does that have to do with anything?" Later, when the group members one by one pledge allegiance to Quill's plan, Groot adds his "I am Groot," and we *all* understand what he means. It becomes a part of the fun to decipher Groot's meaning not on the basis of the words he speaks but on context, mind reading, and social schemas of conversation.

What does all this imply about fantasy? We have seen that the depiction of animated faces—even those that are caricatures—relies on a tacit knowledge of human responses to the face and thus on correspondences between the depicted face and the appearance of actual human and animal faces. In *Guardians of the Galaxy*, we see a similar dynamic in relation to social convention and intuitive psychology. While this planning scene diverges in surprising ways from our expectations regarding such scenes and social conventions, these divergences rely on a backdrop of "the normal" to function. Fantasies connect with us because in fundamental ways they correspond with our everyday worlds; they intrigue us, however, in the ways that they diverge. The mixture of correspondence and divergence can be powerful indeed.

CULTURAL MEMES AND *WONDER WOMAN*

Fantasy films feature stories that are firmly grounded in common human experience and that also align with the values, perspective, enthusiasms, and structures of feeling of a place and time. To illustrate this, consider *Wonder Woman*, a story with a character born of the comics and since then resurrected in several screen and television adaptations. *Wonder Woman* stars Gal Gadot as Diana Prince, aka Wonder Woman. Diana is an Amazon warrior, the Amazons being a tribe created by Zeus to protect humankind. Diana is raised on the hidden island of Themyscira, where she is kept from knowing her true identity as the daughter of Zeus and Queen Hippolyta, thus being an immortal goddess herself. When a World War I pilot, Captain Steve Trevor (Chris Pine), crashes his plane off the coast, Diana saves his life. She learns that a great war (World War I) is consuming the outside world and determines to go there, find Ares, the god of war, subdue him, and stop the war. Along the way to her eventual victory over Ares and the war's end, Wonder Woman has plenty of opportunities to display her ample fighting skills and to become romantically involved with Captain Trevor.

The literary theorist Patrick Colm Hogan finds that two of the most common types of stories to appear cross-culturally are the romantic tragicomedy and the heroic tragicomedy, each type rooted in a universal human concern, the attainment of which is thought to bring happiness. The first concern is the attainment of romantic union and the second the attainment of power (Hogan 76–121). *Wonder Woman* channels both of these concerns, combining elements of both narrative types.

With regard to *romantic union*, Diana and Steve are thrown together when, after Diana saves him from certain death by drowning after his plane crash, their goals at least partially align and they engage on a common quest to visit the arena of World War I. Diana's goal is to locate and kill Ares, the god of war, and bring peace to the world. Steve knows nothing of Ares but wants to infiltrate the German command and stop the production of a dangerous poison gas. Since Diana is unfamiliar with the world of men, the two engage in lots of suggestive banter and eventually fall in love and spend the night together. Diana later becomes enraged at Steve when he apparently stands in the way of her goal to kill Ares because he wishes to destroy the poison gas. But later she understands his motivations, especially after he gives his own life to destroy the gas and thereby saves countless human lives (more on this later).

The other common human concern embodied in this story is the *attainment of power*. The fact that both Diana and Steve have goals that the spectator can ethically affirm does not diminish the fact that both must attain power to reach these goals. Steve is a spy who uses his guile to infiltrate enemy lines, while Diana, naïve in the ways of the outside world, gradually discovers her powers as a goddess, which are constantly and effectively put on display in the film. She leaps high into second-story buildings, deflects bullets with her wrist guards, and defeats Ares and many others in deadly hand-to-hand combat.

It is important to realize what is going on here for the spectator at a psychological level. Viewers form allegiances with both Diana and Steve, aligning their desires with the character's needs and goals. Thus, it brings viewers pleasure when the two characters form a romantic union and when their goals are achieved. For this reason, the pleasures that the film elicits depend on the assumption that viewers share a common orientation toward romantic union and the attainment of power and that, once viewers form allegiances with both Diana and Steve, they will desire those things for the favored protagonists. *Wonder Woman* corresponds with everyday reality, in that it affirms these things, presuming them to be features of the viewer's everyday psychological reality. This fantasy film is firmly grounded in normal, everyday human desires.

These basic human desires are always put into a more culturally specific context, however. Our everyday reality is organized by dominant religions, mythologies, political and social thought, cultural memes, structures of feeling, and various other cultural commonplaces. Two of the most obvious in *Wonder Woman* are the Christ story and feminism. First, *Wonder Woman* is clearly a Christian allegory. A quick internet search will demonstrate that scores of critics—both religious and secular—have noticed this. Diana is something of a Christ figure, or in other words, a character whose life and behavior imitate or resonate with those of Jesus Christ. Like Christ, Diana is both human and god, being the daughter of the god Zeus and the Amazon Hippolyta. Jesus is incarnated on Earth as both God and man to redeem the world; that is his mission and purpose. Diana also takes on a redemptive mission as both goddess and Amazon; she leaves her idyllic island to enter the fray of World War I to defeat evil and to bring lasting peace to the planet. Her evil brother, the god Ares, tries to convince her that the humans are not worth saving, a clear parallel with Jesus's temptations by Satan. But Diana claims that she "believes in love" and that such love does not depend on what we deserve. This echoes the Christian idea that God "is love," that God grants undeserving sinners grace, and that Jesus was sent to save humanity because "God so loved the world" (John 3:16). Both Wonder Woman and the Christ story, then, affirm a forgiving love as the cardinal human virtue. Then there is, of course, the central facet of the Christ story, his sacrifice of his own life for the sake of humanity. Although Diana does not sacrifice her life as Jesus does, the idea of sacrifice is displaced onto two parallel characters. The first is Diana's mentor and aunt, General Antiope (Robin Wright), who takes a bullet to save Diana, thus sacrificing her life for the sake of Diana and her mission. Steve also becomes a sacrificial figure. At the story's end, Steve flies a bomber filled with the poison gas high into the sky and blows up the plane, releasing the poison gas so high in the atmosphere that it poses no threat to the humans on the Earth below. Thus, he sacrifices himself to save the lives of others. The Christ story is a powerful influence in Western and other cultures, for both Christians and others. *Wonder Woman*, then, intersects with and draws from the power of the Christian story and its narrative of sacrifice, redemption, and the importance of love.

The film also draws from the power of cultural movements that are more recent in origin. Most importantly, its narrative plays to a culture concerned with issues of gender equality and feminism. The film has generated debate about its representation of female power and the female action hero. On the one hand, Gal Gadot's Wonder Woman is strikingly beautiful and sexualized, with several of the male characters commenting on her looks. Her costume is clearly designed to highlight her physical features and has thus become a target of feminist critique. This criticism of the film emerges from long-standing feminist concerns with the depiction of women as sexual objects rather than as fully developed persons. This aspect of the film seemingly exemplifies Laura Mulvey's argument, in her famous article "Visual Pleasure and the

Narrative Cinema," that mainstream movies favor the sexualized male gaze and orient themselves toward male pleasure, turning the woman into an object of desire. On the other hand, Diana emerges from an island of powerful and independent women, demonstrating the possibilities of sisterhood. And far from a passive object of male desire, she is clearly the active hero that moves the story forward. The film turns tables on the conventional cliché of males rescuing females, as Diana not only saves Steve from certain drowning in the ocean after his plane crashes but also destroys the powerful Ares, brings an end to the world war, and saves the world both literally and figuratively. Other aspects of characterization in the film also promote gender equality. The evil scientist figure in science fiction is typically a male. In *Wonder Woman*, however, it is Dr. Poison (Elena Anaya), who concocts the gas that threatens to destroy humanity. *Wonder Woman* could be seen as affirming a postfeminist assumption that women can be both sexually alluring *and* powerful and independent agents, which is itself something of a contentious idea. Critics such as the *Guardian*'s Zoe Williams, in a review entitled "Why *Wonder Woman* Is a Masterpiece of Subversive Feminism," ably highlight the film's contradictions in relation to feminist concerns. Nonetheless, Williams writes that she loved the film not as a guilty pleasure but "with her whole heart."

As of this writing, *Wonder Woman* has made roughly $822 million at the box office internationally, with about half of that coming in the United States. A blockbuster such as this must find a way to embody the wishes, fears, beliefs, and concerns of the masses of people to whom it appeals. It does not need to perfectly embody any ideology or belief system but rather need only allow viewers of diverse nationalities, religions, and ideologies to find points of contact—characters and narratives that represent valuations, ideas, and structures of feeling already existent to them in their everyday worlds. Although fantasy films can inspire us with stories of impossible beings and strange environments, their foundations are still firmly planted on the ground, in this quotidian world in which we all live.

3

SUBJECTIVE REALITIES

Chapter 1 describes realism in film; the chapter argues that despite claims that the movies are a medium that photographically captures the realities of the world, film is a composite (rather than simply a photographic) medium and all films are products of the human imagination. Chapter 2 shows that fantasy films, which are clearly the products of human imagination, must maintain points of contact with the actual world to connect with audiences. Realism and fantasy are less divided than is sometimes thought. This chapter turns to one of the medium's truly remarkable capacities—its ability to both expressively represent and offer spectators a semblance of subjective human experience.

A subjective experience is the experience of an individual or group consciousness. It may be of dreams, premonitions, illnesses, memories, intoxication, drug use, reveries, imaginations, and/or hallucinations. The film medium can expressively capture what it might be like to be a soldier in combat on D-Day, to be lost in the woods in the Pacific Northwest, to be a female FBI trainee in a world of male recruits, to ride one's horse across the Great Plains in the middle of the night under a universe of twinkling stars, or to suffer from "locked-in syndrome," a condition in which one is almost completely physically paralyzed but mentally active. Movies can also represent impossible or deeply strange experiences—what it might be like to fly like Superman, travel into a black hole, or inhabit and share dreams with others, as in the case of *Inception* (2010). We can make a distinction between "subjective realism," the term discussed in chapter 1, and "subjective fantasy" (Campora). While the former attempts to approximate the look and feel of actual human experience, the latter may extend into the realm of the impossible or at least the highly improbable.

Several observers have noted the capacity of the movies to approximate human consciousness. Henri Bergson, the French philosopher and winner of the Nobel Prize in Literature, wrote that the "mechanism of our ordinary knowledge is of a cinematographic kind" (qtd. in Sacks 41). The Harvard psychologists William James and Hugo Munsterberg had similar ideas. Munsterberg wrote one of the world's first important books of film theory, in which he developed the idea of a movie being analogous to the human mind. The film theorist V. F. Perkins describes the movies as "the projection of a mental universe—a mind recorder" (133). But what is recorded or represented is not a mind so much as a conscious, subjective experience of the world. Oliver Sacks writes that a movie, "with its taut stream of thematically connected images, its visual narrative iterated by the viewpoint and values of its director, is not at all a bad metaphor for the stream of consciousness itself. And the technical and conceptual devices of cinema—zooming, fading, dissolving, omission, allusion, association, and juxtaposition of all sorts—rather closely mimic (and perhaps are designed to mimic) the streamings and veerings of consciousness" (41).

If a movie can approximate conscious experience, we should remember that this experience is not merely mental but also resolutely physical. Thus, the sensuous nature of the medium renders consciousness, as I have written elsewhere, not simply as a way of seeing but also as "a way of hearing, feeling, thinking, and responding." The movies offer "a holistic experience connected to the emotions, affects, and the body" (Plantinga, *Moving* 49). Movies can approximate consciousness because they affect the mind *and* the body, or what is sometimes called "embodied cognition." They direct our thoughts but also affect our heart rates and galvanic skin responses. They lead us to anticipate developments and shock us with surprises but also cause us to cry, laugh, and sway with the movements we see on the screen. Movies can elicit emotions and strongly suggest moods and tones. In the cinema, ways of feeling are also ways of thinking.

OBJECTIVE AND SUBJECTIVE NARRATION

Movies usually present events through objective narration. Narration is the process by which the film presents its story to the spectator through structure and style. By ordering events in a certain way and by using various visual and aural strategies in that presentation, filmmakers both tell the story and present a world. A single expressive choice can alter the way that this world is seen or that story is comprehended. Using sad rather than jaunty musical underscoring is one example; relaying story events chronologically rather than through a flashback or flash-forward is another example.

An objective narration presents a world in a way that it conforms to conventional notions of verisimilitude. But what passes for verisimilitude differs depending on the mode of film. In classical Hollywood cinema, objective narration is rooted, as David Bordwell writes, in "a tacit coherence among events" of the narrative and the "consistency and clarity of individual identity" of characters (*Narration* 206). Story events follow each other in a causal pattern that is clear and understandable. Any questions or problems posed by the narration can be expected to have answers or solutions that are plausible according to notions of everyday intersubjective reality. Objective narration facilitates immersion into a fictional world that coheres and makes sense. Character motivations are consistent and fit with intuitive or "folk" psychology (Plantinga, "Folk").

Art cinema develops a different sense of objective narration and verisimilitude. It takes its cue from literary modernism and presents a world that is far less knowable and less beholden to strict causal relationships between events. As Bordwell explains it, art-cinema narration builds scenes "around chance encounters, and the entire film may consist of nothing more than a series of them, linked by a trip . . . or aimless wanderings" (*Narration* 206). Although art cinema presents a different sort of reality, it is still an intersubjective reality in which the world is characterized as aleatory and unknowable and character psychology as uncertain and ambiguous.

Subjective narration, on the other hand, is neither intersubjective nor objective. In other words, its purpose is not to give a sense of the world *out there*, of the world that we intersubjectively experience, that we share with our neighbors or coworkers. Rather, it portrays the world as experienced by an individual (or sometimes a group) in the midst of highly personal and often unusual states of mind. The experience is often idiosyncratic or out of synch with others, perhaps due to drugs, lack of sleep, near-death experiences, mental illness, or the bizarre depths of the human mind in dreams or memories. For that reason, subjective narration is also often restricted; in other words, the narration provides the experience of the character and not of other characters in the (fictional) world. Of course, subjective experience can also be normal and objective. But the kind of subjective narration we are concerned with in this chapter are remarkable experiences, conscious experience as unique, individual, and often somewhat troubling.

In the first few decades of cinema, filmmakers began to experiment with all of the techniques of filmic representation, and especially the camera, to portray subjective experience. In F. W. Murnau's *The Last Laugh* (*Der letzte Mann*, 1924), Emil Jannings plays a proud hotel doorman who loses his job and subsequently his dignity and identity. Karl Freund's cinematography is expressive in communicating the confusion and disorientation that occurs when the doorman's world crumbles around him, using the moving camera, zooming, rack focusing, and various filters and mattes to represent subjective experience. For example, in one scene, the doorman becomes thoroughly intoxicated, and to convey his state, the camera pans left to right, then back again, with Jannings on the same platform as the camera as he seems to wheel about the room.

The French, meanwhile, took these sorts of experiments and made them into a movement that we call French impressionist cinema. After World War I, Paris became the center of an international avant-garde and a home for surrealism, dada, and futurism. Many artists and filmmakers became fascinated with the capacity of this (relatively) new medium to express subjective states such as dreams and illusions. For example, in Germaine Dulac's *The Smiling Madame Beudet* (*La souriante Madame Beudet*, 1923), a woman is caught in a loveless marriage and contemplates killing her husband, who constantly threatens suicide using a revolver during their continual quarrels. Using superimpositions, Dulac shows the woman daydreaming that a handsome tennis player on the pages of a magazine comes to life and throws her miserable husband out of the room. The woman's unhappy subjective state is also communicated by close-ups, split screens and other masking, and close-ups of her husband that use distorting lenses. This capacity of the film medium to provide what Murray Smith calls "subjective access" to the experiences of characters became a focus early in the history of filmmaking (150–52).

The kinds of subjective experiences that movies can represent and approximate are as varied as human subjectivity itself. This chapter focuses on two kinds of subjective experience: memories and dreams.

MEMORIES

The issue of memory and the movies can be approached from various angles. We can speak of the way that movies contribute to *collective* memories, which become solidified (and perhaps confabulated) through myth, ritual, or other forms of collective communication. We could explore the way that the movies form *individual* memories (Zacks 85–112) or else what the movies can teach us about human memory (Seamon). My focus here is on the way that movies represent and provide the virtual experience of individual memories, such as the memory of a childhood experience or of a long-gone romantic partner.

The first principle of representing memory in the movies is that a represented memory needs to be distinguished from the ordinary present. A flashback does not necessarily signify memory, since it could be a flashback to the objective past—what actually happened in the world of the film, as opposed to a subjective memory of the past. Memories must be marked as a character's rumination on or reconstruction of the past, not an intersubjective experience. In Ingmar Bergman's *Wild Strawberries* (1957), we meet an elderly doctor, Isak Borg

(Victor Sjöström), as he travels from Stockholm to Lund, Sweden, with his unhappy daughter-in-law to receive an honorary degree from his alma mater. Along the way, Borg decides to visit the now-shuttered cottage where he spent ten summers as a child.

The most obvious marker of memory is when a character announces in voice-over that he is going to remember. Thus, Borg informs us that when looking at this cottage, his mind was flooded with memories, which are even clearer than reality. A quick dissolve to shots of clouds and wild strawberries together with a harp arpeggio transitions us into Borg's memories of a childhood at this cottage on a lake. That this is an idealized reconstruction of the past is clear from the well-ordered production design and Gunnar Fischer's gorgeous black-and-white cinematography. The costumes are mostly perfectly white, and what appears to be a slight overexposure makes the surfaces positively glisten with reflected light. But even while within Borg's memories, Bergman reminds us that these *are* memories by showing the aged Borg, within the frame, as though he were observing these past events in person. He impossibly stands just around the corner while observing a family meal, his face emerging from the darkness. Or he sits in a field of wild strawberries painfully observing his brother attempt to seduce Sara (Bibi Anderson), Borg's first love.

Of course, in reality Borg was not present to see these things in this way; represented memories are subjective reconstructions, however, not necessarily realist accounts of what actually happened. Toward the end of the film, after Borg has reconciled with his son and daughter-in-law, the old man lies in bed, and we hear his first-person voice-over: "Whenever I am restless or sad during the day, it often calms me to recall memories from my childhood. This is the way it was that night too." The beautiful Sara tells him that she will take him to his "Mama and Papa," because he cannot find them. She takes him by the hand, through a field in the warm sunshine, and leaves him by a perfect view of his parents, who lounge on a hillside just on the other side of a small inlet. Father is fishing, while Mother sews. Father waves at him as the gentle summer breezes warm the air. We see Borg again in a reverse-angle close-up, nostalgically transfixed by this vision of an idealized past.

The second principle regarding the representation of memory is that memories are generally suffused with affect. We tend to remember that which made a significant impression on us. That which impresses us moves us and stands out from the daily progression of ordinary experience. That which we remember is remarkable or extraordinary and thus likely to be accompanied by a strong affective charge. Memories are often tinged with nostalgia for a lost past, as we saw in the final scene of *Wild Strawberries* just mentioned. We also see Borg's painful reminiscences as his brother, Sigfried, seduces Sara. Then later, in a dark hallway, Sara tells a friend that while Borg is "so moral and sensitive" and "talks about sin," Sigfried is "so bold and exciting," and she wants "to go home." Later we learn that Sara married Sigfried and had six children with him. Upon seeing this, Borg remarks that he is "overwhelmed by feelings of emptiness and sadness." Yet his memories help him to see where he has erred in his association with the people around him, to establish a better relationship with his son and daughter-in-law, and to find peace at the film's end. Thus, memories, as we see in *Wild Strawberries*, can range from deeply painful confrontations with one's identity to idealized visions of the best that the world has to offer.

Eternal Sunshine of the Spotless Mind (2004), one of the most remarkable and innovative films ever to examine human memory, is the product of the storytelling imagination of the screenwriter Charlie Kaufman and the visual creativity of the innovative director Michel Gondry. The film begins with a pre-title sequence, when we see Joel (Jim Carrey) waking up in his apartment on a cold winter's morning. He skips work and for some reason (unknown even to him) takes a train to Montauk, where he meets and strikes up a relationship with

Clementine (Kate Winslet), who has also inexplicably traveled to Montauk and the seaside. What they fail to realize at this point is that both of them have previously been in a relationship together but, after various frictions and conflicts, have had their memories erased at Lacuna Inc., with its physician founder Dr. Mierzwiak (Tom Wilkinson). Mierzwiak pinpoints the location of various memories in people's brains by having his patients bring in objects and photographs associated with the person they want to forget. He then uses lasers to zap the brain locations associated with those memories. As Mierzwiak says, "Technically speaking, the procedure is brain damage." Voila! The spotless mind.

Films about memory conventionally use flashbacks and sometimes complex temporal structures that feature flashbacks within flashbacks within flashbacks. *Eternal Sunshine of the Spotless Mind* does feature numerous flashbacks, but the temporal structure of the film is utterly unique. Later in the film, we learn that the pre-title sequence of Joel waking occurs after a night of memory erasing by Lacuna technicians. The scene with the hapless technicians erasing Joel's memory during one drunken night occurred earlier in the story than the pre-title sequence, marking one plot manipulation of story order. But the exterior erasing shots are intercut with the unfolding narrative in Joel's head during the procedure.

The Lacuna technicians erase Joel's memories of Clementine in reverse chronological order, beginning with the most recent and extending backward in time. Thus, the erasure scenes, moving forward in time, are intercut with Joel's memories of Clementine, which move backward in time one by one as they are erased. Distorted and highly stylized as subjective memories would be, these scenes nonetheless reveal the progression of Joel and Clementine's relationship in reverse chronological order. The memories of Clementine become increasingly touching and nostalgic as they move backward toward a time when the two loved each other and were not quarreling.

Though drugged and supposedly sleeping, Joel seems partly conscious of the erasure procedure. In particular, he hears the name "Patrick" repeated over and again. Patrick is the Lacuna employee who is attempting to use "Joel's stuff," earlier collected by Lacuna, to seduce Clementine. Part of Joel's mind rebels against the procedure and attempts to hide his memories of Clementine (which are represented as Clementine interacting with Joel in his own memories) by shuttling her to parts of his mind in which there should technically be no association with her. The scenes inside Joel's head as he fights the procedure are unlike anything ever put on film, as the two characters take on various disguises and run through the landscape of Joel's mind to escape detection. Their attempt to elude the erasure ultimately fails, however, and in a poignant scene in a beach house in Montauk where they first met, suffused with sadness and regret, the last of Clementine is erased from Joel's mind. Just before she disappears, she magically whispers to him, "Meet me in Montauk." Then, later that very morning, the two former lovers, both mysteriously drawn to the location, meet again in Montauk and renew their relationship.

Eternal Sunshine of the Spotless Mind is thematically rich, examining the nature of memory and its relevance to our identities and relationships. But in line with the purpose of this book, which is in part to examine and celebrate the expressive capabilities of the film medium, I will simply note some of the creative techniques Gondry uses to represent the subjective reality in Joel's head during that fateful night. Joel's very last memory of Clementine, which is the first to be erased, is his discussion with a neighbor by the mail slots in his apartment building. As the memory is erased, the neighbor is thrown out of focus, and the lights on him dim to black. The soundtrack features strange tinkling sounds and echoes of distant voices, which suggest that we are entering an alternative universe, the vast world of Joel's mind. The tinkling suggests the breaking of glass, suggesting the shattering of memory, just as the dimming lights suggest memory's disappearance.

The scenes of Joel's memories are often presented first in a traditional realist style. But as the memories near erasure, they become more stylized. Gondry revels in myriad visual and sonic means of depicting memory and its erasure. Backgrounds blur. Visual details, such as the writing on the spines of books, the colors of walls, the facial features of bystanders, and lettering on signs, disappear. As the lighting of memory scenes dims, we are sometimes left with a handheld camera with mounted direct lighting, creating a kind of spotlight effect. The beach house crumbles and deconstructs. A drive-in movie screen disappears. Bystanders at a train station disappear one by one. Gondry uses many practical and in-camera effects, but he also employs CGI, for example, showing an automobile falling from the sky to accent Clem's anger and digitally erasing one of her legs and she walks quickly away from Joel after their last fight.

Various memories blend together in a confusing mixture, signaling both Joel's attempts to make sense of what is happening and the subjective and chaotic nature of memory itself. In one scene, he remembers lying on the frozen Charles River with Clem by his side. After noting his happiness, he says to Clem that this is exactly where he wants to be. Then he and Clem are suddenly lying on concrete with bystanders walking by. He calls out her name as she recedes from him into the darkness, as though pulled by some unknown force. Gondry uses fast motion, reverse motion, distorted voices and sounds effects, filtered light, and other techniques to depict what is going on in Joel's head.

In one scene, Joel follows Clementine as she walks away, determined to leave him after their last bitter quarrel. He follows her as she walks down a city street, the camera panning from left to right, then from right to left as Joel becomes spatially confused and changes direction. No matter which way he walks or turns, he approaches the car that he had earlier parked and walked away from. He also sees Clem walking up ahead of him, first right to left, then left to right. Gondry accomplished this with frame inversions, morphing shots together digitally, and frame-by-frame rotoscoping (tracing over motion-picture footage).

In another famous scene, Joel and Clem have escaped into his childhood memories, and Joel sits beneath the kitchen table during a party. Clem appears as a strange hybrid of Clem and one of Joel's mother's friends, dressed in fabulous 1960s fashion and smoking a cigarette. This scene uses forced perspective to make little Joel (played by the adult Jim Carrey), in his pajamas, appear to be much smaller than Clem (who appears as an adult) in the foreground. Little Joel is also dwarfed by the table, the refrigerator, and the kitchen counter. Later this toying with relative sizes become more extreme, as we see both Joel and Clem taking a bath together in the kitchen sink.

While *Eternal Sunshine of the Spotless Mind* is a fascinating representation of memory, no discussion of memory on film should ignore the psychological thriller *Memento* (2000), directed by Christopher Nolan. *Memento*, however, is less about the subjective experience of memory per se and more about what it might be like to attempt to keep track of and reconstruct the past in the *absence* of memory. The film tells the story of Leonard (Guy Pearce), who attempts to track down the man who he believes raped and murdered his wife. The problem for Leonard is that he suffers from anterograde amnesia, the inability to form new memories. With his short-term memory loss, he resorts to various prompts and tricks to keep him focused on his task and keep track of its progress. Thus, he uses Polaroid photographs, tattoos, and notes to himself to "remember" the events that he will inevitably forget after about five minutes.

If *Eternal Sunshine* immerses us in Joel's mind as he both remembers and fights against erasure, *Memento* provides a version of the confusions that occur when one's short-term memory has completely failed. What we learn is that Leonard is subject to the manipulation of the people around him and cannot reconstruct the past, leading to what seems like the murder of not only an innocent man but also a friend and ally. Ultimately, however, what interests Nolan is not the portrayal of Leonard's subjective mental space but the creation of a puzzle for the viewer. The film alternates between two types of scenes. First are the black-and-white scenes in which Leonard speaks to an unknown caller on the telephone. These progress chronologically forward, ultimately revealing the identity of the caller. The second type are the color scenes, which take up the bulk of the narrative and are shown in reverse chronological order, extending backward in time and revealing to viewers how Leonard got himself into each succeeding predicament. The film presents a real challenge for the viewer in attempting to make sense of this complex plot and construct a coherent story from it. After repeated viewings, many viewers are still left with significant questions. Thus, we call this a "puzzle film," in which the viewer must work to understand a complex plot about an amnesiac who fails miserably to understand his own past and to put his current actions into a coherent motivational context.

DREAMS

Many film critics and theorists have analogized film viewing to dreaming. When we watch a film, we sit in a stationary seat and are somewhat immobile. The lights dim to minimize our awareness of surroundings, and we become immersed in an imaginary world. When the screening ends and the film comes to a close, our consciousness returns to the world around us as though from a state of semisleep, or daydream. Thus, the theorist Jean Mitry writes that the psychological state elicited by film viewing is something midway "between actual dreaming and daydreaming" and something like hypnosis in its "captivation" of the viewer's consciousness (82).

Critics from diverse traditions have noticed the similarities between dreaming and film viewing. For example, one can find a thorough examination of the film-dream analogy by the philosopher Colin McGinn in his book *The Power of Movies: How Screen and Mind Interact*. Still, the film-dream analogy has been of especial interest to those who are influenced by psychoanalysis. For Sigmund Freud, dreams, when properly interpreted, offered glimpses into the deepest recesses of the unconscious mind. Dreams offered signs and symbols that revealed truths about our psyches that were unavailable to conscious introspection. Psychoanalytic film theorists later argued that films had latent, or hidden, content that could be psychoanalyzed like a dream.

Early surrealist filmmakers were strongly influenced by psychoanalysis. The great surrealist artist Salvador Dalí and the filmmaker Luis Buñuel, in their *Un chien andalou*

(*An Andalusian Dog*, 1929), present a loose narrative that embodies the bizarre twists and developments of dreams, with implausible actions linked by free association. We see two priests, each dragging a dead donkey and a piano across the floor of an interior building. We see a man look at a hole in his hand, out of which crawl dozens of ants. To take another famous example, Maya Deren's surrealist film *Meshes of the Afternoon* (1943) prominently displays Freudian symbols, such as the knife or the flower, that beg to be interpreted from a psychoanalytic perspective. In Buñuel's later film *The Discrete Charm of the Bourgeoisie* (*Le charm discret de la bourgeoisie*, 1972), he humorously riffs on the cliché of "waking up from a dream" when he ends his film with several characters successively waking from nightmares, implying that the film we have just seen is a dream within a dream within a dream and so on. And Salvador Dalí was hired by Alfred Hitchcock to produce the famous dream sequence in Hitchcock's film *Spellbound* (1945), a sequence exhibiting surrealist conventions of mise-en-scène and the sorts of symbols associated with psychoanalysis—scissors, a man with no face, multiple eyes that suggest voyeurism, curtains, falling, being chased, and so on.

If a film is particularly well suited to represent embodied human experience, it is also suited to represent dreaming. The dream sequence has become a staple of narrative film, with such sequences clearly demarcated from waking life that is depicted in the traditional realist style. Dream sequences call for all types of expressive techniques to depict the strange landscape of dreams and dreaming. As Bordwell notes, dreams are often "rendered as either diffuse, soft-focused reveries or harshly lit special-effects nightmares" (*Christopher* 33). An example of the latter is the initially jokey but eventually nightmarish dream sequence in *The Big Lebowski* (1998), in which the "Dude" (Jeff Bridges) has a drug-induced dream about starring in an erotic film about bowling. The sexualized imagery (for example, phallic bowling pins and sexualized costuming) fits well with psychoanalytic claims about the centrality of libidinal drives in unconscious life. We also see the German nihilists who appear toward the dream's end, carrying giant scissors and evoking Freud's idea of castration anxiety. The sequence contains obvious nods to the disturbing surrealist landscapes of Salvador Dalí in its mise-en-scène. But the Coen brothers also provide a humorous reference to movie history by staging the dream as a sort of Busby Berkeley musical, with a troupe of women in elaborate bowling-themed costumes performing choreographed movements. As Bordwell notes, the landscape of cinematic dreams is often "openly unrealistic" and the actions presented "illogical and implausible" (*Christopher* 33).

As he did with vanished short-term memory in *Memento*, Christopher Nolan has provided a unique perspective on dreams and dreaming in his *Inception*. *Inception* stars Leonardo DiCaprio as a professional thief who steals information by infiltrating people's subconscious minds through their dreams; he calls this *extraction*. Much more challenging than extraction, however, is the process of *inception*, in which he plants ideas or goals into the mind of his target victim. The story presumes the invention of a technology that allows people to share in each other's dreams; this allows *Inception* to take on the structure of a heist film, in that it is a group of individuals who embark on the dreamy caper together. Cobb is tasked with planting a goal into the mind of a victim; he must convince a media mogul to break up and sell off parts of his media empire. Complicating things is that Ariadne (Ellen Page), the "dream architect" who is brought onto the "dream team" to assist in their caper, realizes that Cobb blames himself for the suicide of his wife, Mal (Marion Cotillard), and part of him wishes to join her in the dreamscape that they had earlier constructed together.

Bordwell writes that the artistic purpose of *Inception* is not "to explore our dream life or theories about it." Rather, "Nolan uses the *idea* of exploring dream life, along with the structure of the traditional caper film, to create a complex narrative experience for the viewer" (*Christopher* 35). As dreams are embedded within dreams, the viewer must navigate between five levels of dream and reality, each with its own subplot. The fantasy worlds of stories often contain numerous rules to ensure that the viewer can understand what is happening and form expectations and anticipations for future events. To make sense of *Inception*, likewise, the viewer also must keep track of the numerous rules governing the shared dreaming technology. For example, up to four levels of dreams can be constructed. Shared dreaming often requires a team, including an Architect, a Monitor (to remain with the machine), a Dreamer (who controls the dream), and a Mark (the subject of the extraction or inception). When sedated, one requires a "kick" or falling sensation to wake up into the next level. Limbo is an unconstructed dream space, shared by anyone who is dreaming at the same time. The complexity is staggering, which, of course, is the point. This is a great example of a puzzle film, the action of which occurs almost entirely in dreams.

Dreams and memories are two of the endless variety of subjective experiences commonly represented in stories on screens. Subjective experiences are firmly a part of the everyday world but nonetheless suggest that people experience that world in vastly different ways. The experience of dreams and memories is often quite bizarre. Perhaps films can make some of those subjective experiences available to the rest of us.

4

RUPTURED REALITIES

The movies demonstrate their expressive capabilities not only in representing subjective experiences like memories and dreams but also in their ability to create "ruptured realities," narrative worlds in which the viewer's assumptions can be subtly or decisively undermined. The story worlds of films are sometimes highly unstable. That can make viewing such ruptured realities quite macabre and shocking. These instabilities can stem from many sources, including unreliable narrators, twist endings, or the mixing of fiction and nonfiction in impossible ways.

These sorts of ruptured realities date back to the early years of film history. One famous example is Robert Wiene's *The Cabinet of Dr. Caligari* (1920), a German silent film in which a young man, Francis (Friedrich Feyér), becomes suspicious of Dr. Caligari (Werner Krauss), a carnival hypnotist who makes a living by displaying a sleepwalker, Cesare (Conrad Veidt), at traveling fairs. Francis begins to suspect Dr. Caligari of foul play, eventually accusing him of manipulating the sleepwalking Cesare to commit murders in the little town of Holstenwall. Viewers instinctively trust Francis, who seems to be a kind and sensible young man when compared with the bizarre-looking Dr. Caligari. In a twist ending, however, we learn that Francis is actually an inmate in an insane asylum and that Dr. Caligari is the asylum's respected director. The story we had been enjoying was in fact the musing of a madman. Or was it? The ending is deliberately left open to audience interpretation.

The sorts of narratives that establish one reality only to rupture it and suggest another, to undermine our sense of verisimilitude, or to suggest fundamental instability of "the real" did not originate on the screen, of course. Sophocles's *Oedipus Rex*, performed for the first time probably in the fifth century BC, features a protagonist who searches for the murderer of his father, only to discover not only that *he* is in fact the murderer but also that he has unwittingly married his mother. These revelations dramatically alter the nature of his quest (and of his entire world) in ways similar to the effect of many more stories featuring ruptures, including the film to be discussed shortly in this chapter, *Shutter Island* (2010).

Although these ruptured realities are not unique to storytelling in the movies, the means by which the worlds and their ruptures are expressed are often remarkable.

The film medium draws from all other art forms, but what is unique about film is not only techniques that are medium specific, such as editing, but also the *combination* of expressive techniques, such as the music that may underscore the visual images or acting combined with digital visual effects. (As we have learned, the film medium is a composite medium.) In *The Cabinet of Dr. Caligari*, the off-kilter world is suggested by the hallmarks of what is now known as the German expressionist style. Here it is in part the acting, which aims not at naturalism but rather at strange and stylized movements, gestures, and facial expressions, together with heavy makeup. The mise-en-scène of the film is also heavily stylized, with sets consisting of backdrops that are misshapen, distorted, and intentionally painterly. In expressionism, inner torment is often expressed through outer forms such as halting movements and distorted imagery.

This chapter, then, examines some of the ways that screen stories have presented ruptured and unstable realities, paying attention in particular to (1) the gradual disclosure of incompatible worlds, (2) dual alternative worlds, and (3) twist endings that demand wholesale reinterpretation of what has come before. The chapter also focuses on medium-specific ways in which these films represent their unstable worlds, the unreliability of their narrators or protagonists, and the reconfigurations made necessary by twist endings. One warning for readers: this chapter features many spoilers, which are in this case necessary to fully examine the ruptured realities these films disclose.

GRADUAL DISCLOSURE

Shutter Island, adapted from Dennis Lahane's novel of the same name and directed by Martin Scorsese, begins in the usual objective realist mode. It presents a recognizable world in which we easily understand the motivations, goals, and intentions of the major characters and have firm expectations about the world in which they live. The reality that is initially established seems firm and stable, though full of foreboding, as signaled by the insistent bass notes of the musical piece *Lontano*, composed by György Ligeti. We first meet the federal marshal Teddy (Leonardo DiCaprio) and his new partner, Chuck (Mark Ruffalo), on a foggy day on a ferry on their way to Shutter Island. Chuck asks Teddy if he has "got a girl," and we get the first flashback to Teddy's memory of his former wife, Dolores (Michelle Williams), who he tells Chuck has passed away. The two are headed for an island on which lies a hospital for the criminally insane, headed by Dr. Cawley (Ben Kingsley). Their purpose is to investigate the disappearance of a patient, Rachel

Solondo (Emily Mortimer), who had allegedly killed her three children.

Only the sharpest viewers will pick up on the earliest clues the filmmakers give us that all is not what it seems. For one, when Teddy and Chuck disembark the ferry onto Shutter Island, the guards seem very hostile toward Teddy, cocking and holding their guns menacingly. It is only later that we learn the source of their hostility. For another, Teddy's partner, Chuck, ostensibly also a federal agent, has trouble getting his firearm out of his holster when asked to disarm. One would think this would be second nature for a seasoned federal marshal. The gradual disclosure of an alternative reality becomes something of a game, as Teddy's increasingly bizarre dreams and hallucinations and the events portrayed through what earlier had been an objective realist narration become increasingly outrageous and unbelievable. At first the narration clearly distinguishes dream and hallucination from reality, but in the film's second act, even what we "objectively" see becomes questionable. What is initially set up is an objective reality, which spectators eventually recognize as not objective at all but rather Teddy's subjective reality, before we are returned to an objective reality that reveals what is *actually* going on.

Throughout the film, we are subjectively aligned with Teddy. He is the constant focus of the camera's attention and is given the most close-ups. We are also granted inter-mittent access to his consciousness. In the first act of the film, we see Teddy's experiences and flashbacks to mem-ories, during which we experience things as he sees them. For example, as he approaches the asylum (for what we believe is his first time), he notices the inmates working in the garden. One old woman in particular catches his attention. In a series of slow-motion point-of-view shots and close-ups as he walks, we see him eye the woman. She is balding, with bloodshot eyes and a scar across her neck. She returns his gaze and puts her finger to her mouth in a gesture of shushing. The dialogue we had been hearing is lowered in the sound hierarchy, while the sounds of birds, crickets, and other ambient noise are raised. This moment of subjectivity is hardly alarming at this point and is prob-ably taken as an expression of Teddy's alarm and perhaps fear in response to this foreboding asylum and its poten-tially violent inhabitants. Teddy also has flashbacks to his experiences at Dachau, where as a US soldier he had wit-nessed the liberation of that death camp and the horrors it revealed. But so far nothing seems alarmingly off-kilter. Teddy is haunted by his strange environment, by his wife's death, and by his traumatic war memories.

During the film's second act, Teddy has to change into an inmate's white garb because his federal marshal outfit has been soaked in the rain. That is his costume for the rest of the story, as it gradually becomes apparent that Teddy is *himself* an inmate of the asylum. He begins to experience migraines, during which bright white light bathes the scene. His dreams and memories become increasingly vivid and bizarre. The scenes of "objective reality" begin to take on aspects of hallucination, with extreme content, surreal lighting touches, or odd framings that suggest that something is skewed.

By the time Teddy decides to investigate the mysterious lighthouse in which he believes nefarious surgical experiments are being carried out, "objective reality" has become so bizarre and events so unbelievable that spectators suspect that this supposedly objective narration is in fact the subjective perspective of man with severe mental problems. He sees Chuck's body at the base of a cliff by the sea, then improbably climbs down the vertical wall, at one point hanging on for dear life after losing his balance. When he reaches the base of the cliff, the body has disappeared. He then sees hundreds of rats emerging from a hole in the cliffs. Then he notices a light high up on the cliff, seeming to emanate from a cave. Again he improbably steps over thousands of rats and climbs the impossibly steep precipice to enter the cave, where he finds a woman who turns out to be the woman whose disappearance he had been investigating. She reveals to him a story about secret experiments, Nazis, and forced imprisonment.

But it is all Teddy's hallucination. Later Dr. Cawley reveals to Teddy that he has in fact been an inmate at the asylum for the past two years. They had been engaging in an elaborate ruse, allowing Teddy to "play" the role he imagined himself occupying, the role of a federal marshal investigating nefarious goings-on, in the hope that by playing the role he would be cured. In fact, Teddy had killed his wife himself after finding that she had drowned their three children, and he had constructed an elaborate fantasy because he was unable to handle his guilt.

In the tradition of mainstream films with satisfying endings, *Shutter Island* returns us to an objective reality when we learn the truth about Teddy. The pseudo-objective world we thought we inhabited at the film's beginning was in fact an elaborate charade staged for Teddy's benefit. By gradually revealing the troubled nature of Teddy's conscious life, the filmmakers also gradually reveal the fissures and instabilities of that world. But by the film's end, we are reassured that the world gradually revealed is in fact stable, knowable, and more comforting than Teddy's subjective nightmares. In the last scene of the film, Teddy allows himself to be taken off to receive a lobotomy, suggesting that his delusions will now end.

WORLDS WITHIN WORLDS

Whereas *Shutter Island* portrays an alternative universe of the mind, and one caused by mental illness, *The Matrix* (1999) suggests that the physical world we all inhabit—whether we are mentally healthy or not—is an illusion. Lurking behind it is a far more sinister reality in which our bodies are used as batteries by advanced machines of our own making and in which our conscious thoughts and experiences are fabrications designed by the machines to keep those batteries content and operational.

In *The Matrix*, the spectator learns about ruptured realities early in the film. In this case, it is the quotidian world of everyday experience that is in fact nothing more than a computer program, the Matrix, designed, as Morpheus (Laurence Fishburne) tells Neo (Keanu Reaves), to be "the world that has been pulled over your eyes to blind you to the truth." The truth is that humans are slaves, born into bondage to serve as living batteries, human fuel cells for the AI machines that have been battling humans for more than a century. As Neo is shown the real world for the first time, we see him in a womb-like pod bathed in life-preserving fluids and connected to several tubes that keep him alive. Then as the camera pulls back, we see that Neo is in fact just one of thousands, perhaps millions, of other humans who live their lives in such pods, all the while immersed in dreams that look a lot like American urban life in the 1990s. As Neo learns later, the first dreams constructed for the humans were too idyllic, causing them to constantly wake up. The dreams designed to replace these original, failed dreams have content that incudes sickness and even death, allowing humans a certain verisimilitude that enables deep, constant sleep.

The differences between *Shutter Island* and *The Matrix* are substantial. In *Shutter Island*, the alternative realities are Teddy's subjective fantasies, fueled by his insanity, versus the rational and comforting objective world in which he is an inmate in the Ashecliffe Hospital for the Criminally Insane. In *The Matrix*, the alternative realities are the Matrix, and the objective world is the one in which humans serve as batteries for machines. Yet while *Shutter Island*, arguably, elicits no strong call for philosophizing, *The Matrix* certainly does. While the gradual disclosure of alternative worlds in *Shutter Island* may be fascinating and complex, *The Matrix* self-consciously wonders whether it is better to be in the Matrix or in the real world. Why choose one over the other? *Shutter Island* teases the viewer with clues that the objective reality set up by the film may in fact be unstable and unreliable. *The Matrix*, on the other hand, reveals its dual worlds quite early in the film so that both characters and viewers can engage in dialectics about the nature of reality, what we can know, and what value we should put on personal pleasure versus the pursuit of freedom and truth.

The Matrix elicits deep philosophical questions that have preoccupied humanity for thousands of years (Grau). Plato wondered if the human lot was to be confined in something like a cave in which shadows from the outside world are cast on the interior cave walls. Having never seen the world outside the cave, the cave dwellers mistake the shadows for reality, not realizing that a real world awaits on the outside. Centuries later, René Descartes wondered how we can know anything at all and whether we could trust our senses. After all, he reasoned, it could be that an evil genius has used all of his power and craftiness to deceive us into mistaking the world around us for reality. More recently, the "brain in a vat" scenario is commonly used in philosophical thought experiments to explore conceptions of reality, truth, consciousness, and meaning. And it is precisely the fact that the ruptured reality is revealed early in the film that makes *The Matrix* so philosophically interesting. For one thing, it allows the characters themselves to discuss the issues raised by their predicament, or at least to make statements ripe for philosophical discussion. The character Cypher (Joe Pantoliano), for example, chooses the Matrix over the real world. While chewing on a piece of steak, he knows that it is only his brain that is telling him that it is juicy and delicious but says that "ignorance is bliss." Then later, as he murders some of his compatriots, he says that he thinks "the Matrix can be more real than this world."

When Neo is first shown the nature of reality, Morpheus welcomes him to "the desert of the real." One might think that living in the dream world of *The Matrix* would be preferable to the discomforts and dangers of the real world; that is what Cypher comes to believe. Yet *The Matrix* firmly chooses the side of difficult truths and hard realities over the pleasures of fantasy and illusion. And as Colin McGinn notes, for Neo, Morpheus, and most of the crew of the ship *Nebuchadnezzar*, "freedom from the Matrix takes on the dimensions of a religious quest" (63). Neo, the "One," becomes the Christ figure, sent to rescue humanity from the machines. Morpheus is the John the Baptist figure, preparing the way for the coming of the One. Cypher is a Judas figure, betraying Neo and Morpheus in return for creature comforts. As in *Wonder Woman*, fantasy has roots in prior stories that have deep significance for humanity.

The Matrix draws a sharp distinction between the Matrix and the actual world. And it uses many traditional filmic means to distinguish between those worlds. One such technique is the coloring of the two worlds. The Matrix has a green tint throughout, echoing the cascading green Matrix code that characters observe on computer screens. The tinting is somewhat eerie and artificial, and some viewers have suggested it mimics the look of computer screens of the 1990s. Reality, on the other hand, is coded blue and gray. Since in the war with the machines, humans had earlier eliminated sunlight (by causing something like a "nuclear winter"), the real world is always dark with blue and gray tints. The exception to this is the scene when Neo wakes up to his true state, hooked to a life-support system in a pod among thousands of others. The pods glow red amid a sea of blacks and grays, perhaps signifying the life-preserving fluids in which the human battery cells are immersed. Cypher agrees to help the machines capture Morpheus in return for a life in the Matrix, where he will be granted riches and power. As he kills some of his compatriots, he tellingly wears a red shirt that is out of place in the bluish grays of the real world.

Yet if these alternative realities are sometimes distinguished by traditional cinematic techniques, *The Matrix* also makes use of (what were in the 1990s) cutting-edge technologies to portray the world of the Matrix. Neo must undergo training to learn how to combat the sentient machines that pursue him in the Matrix; Morpheus and Trinity (Carrie-Anne Moss) have already undergone this training and are able to perform physical feats not seen in the actual world. Thus, at the film's beginning, we see Trinity fighting the police and sentient machines that come for her. She has seemingly superhuman martial arts skills and lighting-quick movements, sometimes displayed in extreme slow motion. She can run horizontally across walls. She can jump from building top to building top and fly through windows seemingly unhurt. As one cop remarks, "That's impossible."

During the climactic fight against the sentient machines on a building top, both Trinity and Neo display skills that could occur only in the alternative world of the Matrix. But Neo's skills begin to match those of the machines, as he defies the laws of physics to move out of the way of bullets shot at him by the sentients. As Trinity says, "I've never seen anyone move that fast." This is portrayed using a technology later dubbed "bullet time," or time-slice photography, used to slow down the pace of an action scene to extreme slow motion. The technique is made possible by the use of dozens of still cameras that surround the subject and are timed to photograph the subject sequentially depending on the desired effect. In the scene in question, time is slowed down to the extent that the audience can see the path of the bullets as they speed toward Neo. This constitutes a particularly cinematic means of portraying the strange physics of an alternative world.

TWIST ENDINGS

While *The Matrix* reveals ruptured worlds early in the narrative, some screen stories withhold full knowledge of the ruptures until the very end. In *Planet of the Apes* (1968), the astronaut Taylor (Charlton Heston) and two compatriots crash into a lake on an unknown planet, after having spent an unspecified time in hibernation on their long-distance space voyage. Traveling at nearly the speed of light, they have aged only eighteen months. A fourth astronaut has died during the flight due to a malfunction. After some exploration and a strange encounter with a tribe of primitive humans, they are captured by a group of gorillas on horseback, and some of their wounds are treated by chimpanzee doctors. In this world, they soon discover, various species of apes are at the apex of animal development. It is the apes that are apparently advanced and intelligent, while Homo sapiens are considered to be primitive and unintelligent—in short, beasts or animals. Taylor spends much of his time on this strange planet trying to convince skeptical apes that he is in fact a sentient being who equals them in intelligence. At one point when he is threatened with castration, he escapes and takes refuge in a museum. There he sees a fellow astronaut and former colleague's stuffed and eyeless corpse on display.

The fictional world created in this film is of course *already* an alternative reality and one that might cause us to question our own. Like many of the sequels that it inspired, *Planet of the Apes* asks us to consider implications about relationships between species in our own world. In this way, it functions as a kind of philosophical thought experiment. The films elicit sympathy for apes, if only by suggestion that apes in our reality occupy the place of the oppressed humans in the films. *Planet of the Apes* has the capacity to generate imaginative thought with genuine ethical significance. If we consider the ape treatment of humans in this film to be somehow wrong, could it be that our actual treatment of apes (and other animals) is similarly wrong?

The ending of *Planet of the Apes*, however, is a twist ending and causes us to question the nature of the world that has been created with skillful verisimilitude. (The original *Planet of the Apes* was praised for the elaborate makeup and costuming required to represent the apes.) Taylor and his newfound human companion, Nova (Linda Harrison), ride a horse along the coast after having escaped their ape captors, suggesting a new Adam and Eve and a possible new humanity. They come across a landmark, however, that causes Taylor to sink to his knees in despair. It is the ruins of a huge sculpture. It is at this point that Taylor first realizes that he is "back."

"I'm home," he says. He realizes what has happened. "You finally really did it," he says in anguish. "You maniacs! You blew it up!" Then he damns the people responsible to hell. The camera tracks back to reveal the ruins of the Statue of Liberty, which has informed Taylor that he is not on some alien planet but back on the Earth. He is now far into the future in comparison with the moment he began his mission, long after an apparent nuclear holocaust has fundamentally altered the nature of life on Earth.

Alternative realities can be revealed through twist endings like the ending of *Planet of the Apes*. This sort of ending reveals new information that causes viewers to radically reinterpret everything that has come before, even to the extent that the very fabric of the portrayed universe seems to have fundamentally changed. Such twist endings are not uncommon in feature filmmaking. Examples more contemporary than *Planet of the Apes* would include Bryan Singer's *The Usual Suspects* (1995), M. Night Shyamalan's *The Sixth Sense* (1999), David Fincher's *The Fight Club* (1999), and Alejandro Amenábar's *The Others* (2001).

In television, excellent examples of the twist ending can be found in several episodes of the much-loved science-fiction series *The Twilight Zone* (1959–64), created by Rod Serling (who also penned an early version of the screenplay for *Planet of the Apes*). The series billed itself as a program that explored the human imagination. Several of the series' episodes feature "snapper endings" with "O. Henry twists." These endings can be categorized according to the way in which they surprise the audience (Plantinga, *Screen* 217–30). *The Twilight Zone* offers both character surprises and spectator surprises; surprises of prospects and surprises of understanding; sudden resolutions of ambiguity or quickly altered frames of reference; and both elevating and deflating surprises.

An example of a sudden resolution of ambiguity occurs in the director Richard Donner's "Nightmare at 20,000 Feet" (1963) from a screenplay by Richard Matheson, in which Robert Wilson (William Shatner), having spent the past six months in a mental institution, is flying back home with his wife, ostensibly having been cured. During the flight, he sees some sort of monster or gremlin hacking away at the wing of the plane during a storm. The trouble is that no one else has seen this gremlin, and given Robert's history of mental illness, no one is inclined to believe him, including most viewers. Does he really see a gremlin, or are these the paranoid rantings of a madman? As Robert becomes increasingly unhinged, the passengers and crew eventually have to restrain him. After landing, Robert is strapped to a gurney, and his wife tells him, "It's all right now, darling." The camera tilts up to serious damage on the wing on which Robert had seen the gremlin, removing all ambiguity in a surprising way. Apparently everything is *not* all right.

RUPTURED REALITIES AND ETHICS

Media makers use moving-image media to create both objective and subjective realities and then in some cases to rupture those realities through the gradual disclosure of a very different reality, the representation of two or more incompatible worlds or twist endings that demand that viewers reinterpret everything they have seen. The rise of puzzle films in the past few decades makes it abundantly clear that many viewers thoroughly enjoy the mental challenge of difficult films that tax their cognitive capacities, that present them with alternative universes or twist endings that call for a complete cognitive reset (Kiss and Willemsen). So these imaginative ruptured realities are fascinating and (not to put too fine a point on it) simply fun.

What about the ethics of ruptured realities? In chapter 1, we discussed the ethics of realism, where we learned that some film theorists have suspected that realist films, films with verisimilitude, have the capacity to convince audiences of their reality when in fact they are merely representations, merely one perspective on the world among many. Realist films may thus have a rhetorical, persuasive power. They invite spectators to become immersed, offering the promise of a reward such as narrative pleasure, while at the same time suggesting powerful perspectives on and attitudes toward what they display in the narrative (Plantinga, *Screen* 11–74). While fiction films are made up, and while fictional characters do not actually exist, the stories in which they appear nonetheless suggest general truths about the world, about what types of people are like (which can lead to stereotypes) or about how a conversation typically goes (as seen in the case of the planning session in *Guardians of the Galaxy*) or about a position on a common cultural meme such as feminism (as seen in *Wonder Woman*).

For this reason, it might be thought that ruptured realities should be lauded from an ethical perspective because they shake us out of our mental doldrums, showing us that the world could be radically different than it is or that our current perspective on the world may be problematic or perhaps completely wrongheaded. What seems to be sanity may actually be madness (*Shutter Island*). What seems to be an objective reality is actually a nefarious illusion (*The Matrix*). What at first glance appears to be an alien world is in fact the Earth of the distant future (*Planet of the Apes*). The poet and playwright Bertolt Brecht, who has had a significant influence on film theory, distrusted spectator immersion because it mystified spectators, making them think that what they were seeing was natural, simply the way things are. Brecht and subsequent film theorists influenced by Brecht favor narratives that confront the spectator with inconsistencies, contradictions, and alienating effects that break the spell of immersion and shake us up (Koutsourakis).

We could praise the kind of films discussed in this chapter as just the sort of film that encourages mental elasticity and epistemic humility, that teaches us that our worldview is subject to radical revision, that our beliefs and attitudes are provisional, that there is always the possibility that our personal "realities" may be ruptured in favor of a new way of seeing the world and our place in it. This blanket endorsement of films with ruptured realities would be premature, however. While the mental gymnastics encouraged by these films does seem salutary, we also need to consider the sort of rupture each film features, the reality being ruptured and presumably left behind, the reality that replaces it, and the cultural context in which the rupture and replacement occur. In other words, ethical considerations need to take into account each individual film within its cultural context.

For example, *The Matrix* might be thought to encourage critical thinking, in that it fosters the idea that the world around us is an illusion that masks a more insidious reality that is hidden and visible only to a few. But consider today's cultural context, in which conspiracy theories run rampant, people distrust official news sources, and there is no version of reality generally accepted as real or accurate. Films such as *The Matrix* could be seen as feeding into a penchant for the acceptance of all sorts of wild conspiracy theories.

In this context, ethics clearly demands that we look a bit closer. A film with ruptured reality is ethically beneficial not merely for suggesting that a rupture is possible but for the type of rupture it suggests and the means portrayed for its discovery. *Planet of the Apes* creates a world in which it is the apes that are at the apex of animal evolution, and humans, for the most part, are primitives who behave like beasts. In that context, is it discovered that Taylor and his associates are intelligent, sentient beings that deserve to be granted rights and respect? It is interesting to note that ape society in the film is governed by a caste system in which the gorillas serve in the military and as laborers, orangutans serve as religious and political leaders, and chimpanzees serve as doctors and scientists. It is a psychologist and an anthropologist who first begin to sympathize with Taylor and Nova and free them to enter the Forbidden Zone, where they escape the forces that are threatened by the truth and wish to treat them like vermin. Thus, it is scientific observation together with a kind of interspecies empathy that recognizes that the humans deserve ethical treatment. The "snapper" ending, the twist that reveals that this world is in fact Earth, suggests that humanity has succeeded only in obliterating the world through nuclear war and that traditional forms of liberal humanism have failed miserably. Perhaps something new must take its place? This brief discussion of the ethics of films with ruptured realities is clearly only a beginning. The general point, however, is clear. The ethical implications of such films depend on their individual characteristics in their particular contexts.

5

DOCUMENTARY:
ART OF THE REAL?

Documentaries have enjoyed a tremendous resurgence of interest in the past few years. More than fictional movies, documentaries are supposedly the art of reality. Yet what they make entirely clear is that there exist innumerable ways to *represent* that reality. Like fictions, documentaries may make use of photographic images and recorded sounds but are still composite, rhetorical, expressive, and creative. Documentaries can be as imaginative as the wildest fantasy film. The classic Barbara Kopple documentary *Harlan County, U.S.A.* (1976), which follows a coal miner's strike in Harlan County, Kentucky, operates in the way most viewers would expect a documentary should. Its motion-picture photography consists almost solely of images used to document the world, as the camera records interviews, meetings, the coal-mining process, and tense confrontations between strikers and "scabs."

Some of the music is diegetic, as we hear actual miners singing about the travails of this dangerous occupation. The nondiegetic musical underscoring is authentic to the time and place. The film is structured in chronological order, such that the viewer can easily follow the events of the strike and its aftermath. *Harlan County, U.S.A.* does what a documentary is supposed to do, which is to use images and sounds to provide the viewer with powerful visual and sonic documents incorporated within a representational structure, together providing deep insights into its subject matter.

Other films we call documentaries, however, raise problematic and interesting issues for this mode of media making. Joshua Oppenheimer's *The Act of Killing* (2012), for example, follows several Indonesian gangsters as they re-create the political killings they perpetrated during a time of political unrest in Indonesia, using elaborate set pieces and makeup. One scene has the gangsters posing in a verdant natural setting before a beautiful waterfall, dancing and singing along with elaborately costumed women. Or take Ari Folman's *Waltz with Bashir* (2008), in which the director interviews several former compatriots about their experiences during the 1982 Israeli invasion of Lebanon to attempt to reconstruct his own traumatic memories of his experience there. The film is almost entirely animated. The film's title is drawn from one scene in which a crazed Israeli soldier dances on a street as snipers fire at him, while in the background we see a huge poster of Bashir Gamayel, the Lebanese president whose assassination indirectly led to the Shabra and Shattila massacre, the aftermath of which is shown in the news footage that is the only footage *not* animated and that ends the film.

The relationship between films we call documentaries, films that mix fiction and nonfiction such as docudramas, and mock documentaries is complex and interesting (Plantinga, "Documentary"). These relationships are the focus of this chapter, with an emphasis on the "mock" or parodic documentary, which it turns out is actually a fascinating and usually humorous kind of fiction film— another alternative reality.

THE DOCUMENTARY CONTRACT

When we watch a film, we want to know what kind of reality it refers to or represents. How do viewers know that they are viewing a documentary rather than a fiction film? Typically films are "indexed" as either fiction or nonfiction. When you sit down to watch *Blackfish* (2013), Gabriela Cowperthwaite's film about Sea World and orca whales, you typically already know that the film is a documentary. You may have read publicity or reviews or heard your friends talking about the film as a "documentary." You may have seen a trailer that uses the same word "documentary." The trailer would probably also feature filmmaking techniques that are strongly associated with the documentary, like handheld camera shots, interviews with experts or witnesses, news or archival footage, and authoritative voice-over narration purporting to give you the truth. In these and other ways, films are usually "indexed," or in other words, identified, as either documentary or fiction or some hybrid between the two (as in the case of docudrama). Indexing can occur in publicity, reviews, or trailers or may be signaled in the film itself (typically at the beginning). Indexing lets us know what sort of work we are viewing (Carroll, *Theorizing* 232; Plantinga, *Rhetoric* 15–21). It also lets us know how we ought to see the relationship between the film and the actual world. Fiction is purportedly about imaginary beings and incidents, though as we have seen, fiction relates closely to the world around us. And documentaries are purportedly "about" the real world, though as I argue, documentaries are also imaginative representations.

What does that mean, this phrase "about the real world"? One thing this does *not* mean is that the documentary is a transparent, unmediated recording of reality. No documentary film could attain this status. A surveillance video is the closest form I can think of to an unmediated record of some small patch of reality. All documentaries are much more heavily mediated than surveillance videos. Documentarians usually incorporate into their finished work only a fraction of the footage they actually take; that choice of footage is mediation. Then the footage is put into an order through editing, thus giving the documentary a structure. This is further mediation. We might add interviews (which involve the choice of subjects to be interviewed), underscoring, voice-over narration, various reenactments, titles and credits, and so on. Documentaries are structured, mediated, created discourses that make an argument, however implicit that argument might be. All documentary filmmaking involves the work of the human imagination.

Critics and even documentary filmmakers have forgotten this point at various times, as some of what was said about the direct cinema movement showed. Direct cinema in the United States, what was called cinema verité in France, and similar developments in Canada caught fire among documentarians in the 1960s after filmmakers and technicians had worked together to develop new, lightweight filmmaking equipment. For the first time, it was possible to synchronize separate sound recorders and cameras without a physical connection through "crystal synchronization." Thus, a two-person crew could take a handheld, shoulder-mounted 16 mm camera and a Nagra tape recorder into the field and "capture a scene" like had never been possible before. In *Primary* (1960), Robert Drew, Ricky Leacock, and the "Drew Unit" recorded and photographed Senators Robert F. Kennedy and Hubert Humphrey, both campaigning in Wisconsin for the Democratic presidential nomination. With their new lightweight equipment, they were able to weave through the crowds, get up onstage with the candidates, spontaneously frame and reframe shots to follow the action and reactions, and produce, in the historian Erik Barnouw's words, an "astonishing," "scintillating and illuminating" documentary account of the campaign (237–38).

Few people had seen anything like this before, and among the filmmaking community, this new way of making films understandably generated a good deal of excitement and led to a new but brief "movement." Direct cinema embraced an ethos of authenticity and an insistence that the filmmaker should observe the world rather than comment on it. At its most extreme, direct-cinema filmmakers insisted that through the finished film, reality should "speak for itself." While many filmmakers were careful to distance themselves from such claims, some fed into this new conception of the documentary as a mere recording, transparent record, or document of reality. And this idea was amplified by various critics, film theorists, and philosophers, some of whom used the impossibility of this supposed documentary replication of reality to claim that all films are fiction films. The ideal or pure documentary becomes the surveillance video. As the philosopher Noël Carroll notes, "Direct cinema opened a can of worms and got eaten by them" (*Theorizing* 225).

This idea of a documentary as a recording, transparent record, or document of reality, flawed though it is, is understandable. After all, documentaries make use of moving photographic images. And individual images may certainly be documents. The moving photograph bears an indexical bond to the real world, in that it is produced by a machine (the camera) in some ways independent of human subjectivity. Thus, images of nature are at the heart of nature documentaries; we can learn a great deal about snakes by seeing images of them—what they look like, how they move, how they strike. Another example would be *Hoop Dreams* (1994), the classic documentary about two boys who have dreams of becoming basketball stars in the NBA. Without the images of the boys at home and on the basketball court, the film would not be so compelling and the information it provides so rich.

Yet despite the importance of motion-picture photography, no documentary is a mere document. Documentaries are neither transparent nor mere recordings.

The first hypothesis we examined in chapter 1 is that all films, whether documentary or fiction, are rhetorical constructs and products of the filmmakers' vision and perspective. More importantly, the third hypothesis examined in chapter 1 holds that the film medium is not inherently a photographic medium. As Stephen Prince argues, the "photographic biasing and the live-action biasing that have existed in generations of thought and theory about the movies have tended to deflect attention from the extent to which cinema is a composited collage of different ingredients" (23). To this we might add that even documentaries composed almost solely of moving photographic images are composites, in the sense that while each individual photograph might be considered to be a document, the hundreds or thousands of individual shots must be assembled and given a broad structure. That assemblage and that structure constitute a kind of theory or account that is a product of the filmmakers' imaginations. It may be more or less accurate, but it is a subjective account nonetheless.

It is for this reason that, as I have argued elsewhere, digital photographs and even "deep fakes" are less threatening to the documentary than is sometimes supposed. A documentary like Louie Psihoyos's *The Cove* (2009) depends on the evidentiary status of photography for its force. It shows images of dolphins being slaughtered in a small cove in Japan, a practice that the local fishermen wished to keep secret. These images seem to prove that at least this particular slaughter actually took place. But what if through digital image manipulation such images could be faked? "Deep fakes" are manipulated videos and audio recordings that look and sound just like the real thing. Software that uses complex algorithms allows even talented amateurs to make videos that appear to show a celebrity or politician saying damning words they would never use in real life. It will probably become increasingly difficult to judge the authenticity of videos that are used in news footage and documentaries.

Does this spell the death of documentary filmmaking? Not really; nonfiction books have never relied on images as evidence, and we still (sometimes) believe them. If visual images are no more reliable than words, we still could invest trust in them under certain conditions. Moreover, not all images in documentaries are used as evidence. Some images are used for informative or illustrative purposes. A drawing of a bird, for example, may be used to show feather patterns or beak size. The drawing may be quite informative despite its being a drawing rather than a photographic image. Documentaries that use images to provide information rather than to serve as evidence of something are not threatened by digital images and the possibility of deep fakes.

Why is that? We often look to the *source* of an article
or documentary or image to determine whether to lend
it credence. Random videos on YouTube will always be
suspect, especially when marshaled for incendiary purposes. But images that have been vetted by trusted news
or information sources, eyewitnesses, or professional
experts may be more reliable. We lend credence to an
image in part on the basis of whether we trust the source
of the image. In the context of persuasive speaking, Aris-
totle wrote of the "ethos" or character of the speaker. All
things being equal, we will be more persuaded by speak-
ers whom we consider to be trustworthy, who seem to
have our interests at heart, and who know what they are
talking about. We often evaluate the source of a documentary, or in other words, the institutional context from
which it emerges, in much the same way.

DOCUMENTARIES AND HYBRIDS

What, then, is a documentary? I propose that we tweak
this question a bit before answering it. Rather than providing a philosopher's definition, let us consider instead
what people usually *consider* a prototypical documentary
to be. When I say "prototypical," I mean that some examples of any category are more central than others. Most
people would agree that robin is a more central example

of the category "bird" than an ostrich is, because a robin can fly and an ostrich cannot. In the same way, some documentaries seem to be prototypical and others not so much. A prototypical documentary would be any episode of the Public Broadcasting System journalistic documentary series *Frontline*, for example, with its authoritative voice-over narrators, clear topical structures, musical underscoring, interviews, and visual images used to illustrate the claims made by what the voice-over and interviewees say. Observational documentaries such as *Harlan County, U.S.A.*, mentioned earlier, or Janus Metz Pedersen's *Armadillo* (2010), which follows Danish soldiers deployed in Afghanistan and avoids all voice-over narration, would also be prototypical documentaries.

My argument is that people usually consider such prototypical documentaries to be "asserted veridical representations" in a moving image medium (Plantinga, "Documentary" 499). If we unpack this a bit further, the phrase is actually not cumbersome or difficult to understand. By "veridical," I mean "truthful" or "accurate." By "asserted veridical," I mean that the documentary is *implicitly claimed or presented as truthful or accurate*. It is not automatically true or accurate. By presenting a film *as a documentary*, the filmmakers affirm that it is a representation they claim should be taken to be true and accurate.

How can this idea be applied to an individual documentary? First, imagine that the voice-over narrator of a documentary about Alaska says something like this: "A chunk of the glacier the size of a house slid into the bay, causing large waves that rocked the boat." In the context of a documentary, this statement is asserted to be true. Now suppose that the scene in question includes a long shot of a chunk of glacier breaking off and falling into the bay, causing large waves that rock the boat. In the context of a documentary, this shot is presented as veridical, or in other words, a trustworthy visual guide to what happened. But an image, it is said, is worth a thousand words. It shows us much beyond what the voice-over narration actually says. It shows us what it looks like when parts of a glacier fall into the water or what it looks like when a boat rocks and passengers on deck frantically try to keep their balance.

Thus, we do not automatically believe everything we see and hear in a documentary, but we do tend to assume that what we are shown and what we hear have been presented in good faith by the makers as an attempt to show and tell the truth. If we cease to believe this, we may accuse the film's makers of being manipulative or dishonest or of having presented blatant propaganda. The makers of such a film have violated the implicit contract between maker and audience that we expect to be honored when people call their work "documentary."

We think of prototypical documentaries, then, as "asserted veridical representations." But what of documentaries that use creative techniques such as animation or reenactments? What about hybrid films that seem to mix fiction and nonfiction? How do these relate to quotidian reality, to the everyday world around us? How do audiences make sense of their relationship to the alternative realities they represent? We should first admit that often audiences do not know how to understand these films vis-à-vis the real world.

Waltz with Bashir, for example, features the actual testimony of former Israeli soldiers as they recount their horrific experiences during the Israeli invasion of Lebanon in 1982. The shots of former soldiers testifying are animated with a combination of traditional 2-D, Flash, and CG techniques. Some scenes simply feature men talking, but others are highly impressionistic. The film begins with a seeming nightmare in which a veteran recalls killing numerous dogs during a mission because they barked and revealed the soldiers' position. Now the dogs, in a pack, run angrily through the streets, knocking over tables and chairs and barking ferociously in a representation of their vengeful rage. In another scene, a soldier floats in the sea on the giant body of a naked woman, a kind of mother

figure. These scenes are clearly representations of subjective dreams or fantasies and take much creative license.
Yet most everyone calls *Waltz with Bashir* a documentary.

To take another example, in *The Act of Killing*, Oppenheimer shows us Indonesian gangsters as they re-create
political killings they perpetrated during political unrest
a few decades ago. The gangsters use heavy makeup
and elaborate sets to reenact those killings. Most of the
gangsters seem to be insensitive brutes, but one gang-
ster is moved to tears and professes to feel sickness and
guilt over his actions. The film also features scenes in
which the gangsters dress in drag or other elaborate costumes and perform for the camera with several dancing
women accompanying them. The film would clearly be
an example of what the film theorist Bill Nichols calls a
"performative" documentary, suggesting that knowledge
is "personal and embodied, rooted in experience, in the
tradition of poetry, literature, art, and rhetoric" (149).
Thus, the relationship between the film and the reality
it depicts is much less straightforward than in a prototypical documentary.

Perhaps the most important type of hybrid film is the
docudrama, a kind of film that lies at the intersection
of fiction and nonfiction. The genre has other names as
well—"dramatic documentary" and "historical fiction,"
for example—that describe its hybrid nature, somewhere

between fiction and nonfiction, traditional drama and the documentary. What makes such films hybrids is that although they purport to be based on true stories or actual historical events, they are scripted, acted, and otherwise carefully constructed in much the same way a fiction film is. Among some well-known US docudramas are Mimi Leder's *On the Basis of Sex* (2018), Spike Lee's *BlacKkKlansman* (2018), Alan J. Pakula's *All the President's Men* (1976), Niki Caro's *North Country* (2005), and the television miniseries *Band of Brothers* (2001).

The fact that the phrase "based on a true story" has become something like a joke is evidence of the skepticism some viewers bring to the supposed "veridical" relationship this genre has with the historical. In this regard, docudramas range from films that attempt to maintain strict historical integrity to those that freely take creative license to alter the story on which they are based. In fact, few docudramas wholly resist the temptation to alter events for dramatic or other creative purposes, providing an opportunity for countless amateur and professional historians to ferret out the inaccuracies. Spike Lee's *BlacKkKlansman*, for example, is based on the 2014 memoir, *Black Klansman*, by Ron Stallworth. Stallworth, the first black cop to serve in the Colorado Springs police force, infiltrated the local chapter of the Ku Klux Klan first on the telephone and then by having a white colleague act as his proxy at actual Klan meetings. In the film, the Klan hatches a bomb plot that is thwarted when the bomb explodes in an unexpected location, killing three members of the Klan. In Stallworth's memoir, there is no such bomb plot. Stallworth did succeed in identifying members of the Klan who were employed by the US military, and they were apparently demoted and reassigned.

Perhaps the most interesting question to be asked of docudramas is not necessarily where their historical inaccuracies lie (though this is important) but rather how the story has been designed for its contemporary audience and what ideological purpose it serves in its contemporary context. In that sense, the historical inaccuracies of Lee's film are far less important than its role in calling attention to racism and Klan activity in US culture. (The film ends with video footage of the 2017 "Unite the Right" rally in Charlottesville, Virginia, at which an antiracism protester was murdered by an individual who intentionally drove his car into a crowd.)

Whatever one thinks about the importance of historical accuracy in the genre, it does seem to be the case that the status of docudramas vis-à-vis history is sometimes confusing. Should audiences see the docudrama as a veridical guide to actual historical events? Skepticism would be advised, but credulity is sometimes the actual audience response. Take Oliver Stone's *JFK* (1991), about the assassination of John F. Kennedy in Dallas, Texas, on November 22, 1963. While the official version of history is that Lee Harvey Oswald acted as the lone assassin, the film suggests a vast conspiracy that involves Cuban gangs, the CIA, and even then–vice president Lyndon Johnson himself. Audiences were unsure about how to take the film. Was it meant to be speculation? A paranoid thriller? A historical account? To make matters worse, Stone constructed the film in a way that blurs the lines between fiction and documentary. The film at times uses traditional color footage and techniques associated with the fiction film, including the steady frame, careful camera movements, classical three-point lighting, and so on. On the other side of the spectrum, Stone uses actual documentary footage of the assassination taken on Super 8 film, the well-known "Zapruder footage." This is "archival" footage of a sort common in documentaries. Then Stone mixes in 16 mm black-and-white footage designed to appear to be documentary footage, with the shaky handheld bounciness, swish pans, and granular imperfections inherent in that gauge of film stock.

Not surprisingly, critics were concerned about how audiences would take the film. Its expertise in filmmaking, creating an immersive and exciting story, might also lead to confusion about the film's historical intentions (Plantinga, *Rhetoric* 22–23). The emotional and dramatic power of docudramas can alter our perspectives and beliefs, even while we consciously realize that they take creative license in representing historical events. This might be especially true if we are confused about the fictional or nonfictional status of a powerful story. Thus, *JFK* caused a great deal of discussion and debate about this very issue (Rockwood).

MOCK DOCUMENTARIES

This Is Spinal Tap (1984) follows the heavy-metal band Spinal Tap, one of "England's loudest bands," as it spirals toward failure and dissolution. As the band descends into oblivion, incessant quarreling causes the band's lead guitarist to depart, and the severely hobbled Spinal Tap ends up playing "freeform jazz" to a bored audience at a minor festival where the band is billed second to a puppet show. The film features the trademarks of the documentary: interviews, handheld cameras that follow the band members at parties or as they walk through the labyrinthine hallways beneath the stages on which they play, and the sort of performance footage that has become the staple of the concert documentary. However much this film appears to be a documentary, *This Is Spinal Tap* is pure fiction. Mock documentaries are fiction films that are designed to look like documentaries and use documentary-style techniques to appear to have the truth-tracking functions of documentary. Unlike documentaries, however, they are wholly scripted and employ actors to play fictional characters. In the case of *This Is Spinal Tap*, the lead guitarist, Nigel Tufnel, is played by Christopher Guest, while the lead singer, David St. Hubbins, is played by Michael McKean. And there was not an actual band called Spinal Tap until Rob Reiner and the cowriting cast members dreamed it up. Later on, after the success of the film, Spinal Tap went on at least two tours. In this case, fiction crossed over into reality.

Mock documentaries, as Jane Roscoe and Craig Hight write, are fiction works in moving-image media "which make a partial or concerted effort to appropriate documentary codes and conventions, in order to represent a fictional subject" (2). Media hoaxes are not mock documentaries, because mock documentaries depend on a knowing viewer. Much of the humor and interest of a mock documentary require a savvy spectator, one who knows what is going on. The mock documentary often wears the mantle of documentary to parody, satirize, or otherwise critically examine its subject. Mock documentaries are also mock indexed as documentaries. In other words, audiences typically know they are not actual documentaries, even while the films appropriate the forms of documentary as a kind of knowing pretense.

Christopher Guest, who cowrote *This Is Spinal Tap*, went on to direct (and cowrite with Eugene Levy) other mock documentaries, and the genre has become something of a specialty for him. These include *Waiting for Guffman* (1996), *Best in Show* (2000), *A Mighty Wind* (2003), and *For Your Consideration* (2006). *Best of Show*, for example, follows several dog owners as they attend a dog show and compete against one another. Guest also directed *Mascots* (2016) for Netflix, a film about mascots competing for the World Mascot Association's Gold Fluffy Award.

Mock documentaries are not necessarily funny but are sometimes dramatically serious. Tim Robbins's *Bob Roberts* (1992), for example, follows the senatorial campaign of a stock trader and folk singer, demonstrating the unscrupulous tactics of dishonest political candidates. Woody Allen's *Zelig* (1983) traces the career of a mysterious shape-shifting man (played by Allen); for the film, Allen's image is edited into historical footage. Mock documentaries have become popular on television as well, with popular comedy series such as *The Office* (2005–13), *Parks and Recreation* (2009–15), and *Modern Family* (2009–20) all made in the mock-documentary style, with swish pans, shaky cinematography, interviews, and knowing glances at the camera.

Many mock documentaries parody the documentary but reserve their satire for something else. Let me explain.

A parody is a kind of imitation, but it does not necessarily imply criticism or even humor. Thus, *This Is Spinal Tap* is a parody of the documentary because it imitates a documentary by using traditional documentary techniques. Satire, on the other hand, *does* imply criticism. Satire has a target, is critical of that target, and works to try to correct it. Thus, while *This Is Spinal Tap* parodies the documentary, it reserves its satire for the peculiar brand of masculine posturing and dumb sexism practiced in heavy-metal rock culture in the late 1970s. The phallic guitars and microphones, tight spandex pants worn by the musicians, and displays of power through "power chords" all demonstrate a kind of juvenile version of masculinity. At the same time, the band performs songs such as "Sex Farm" and "Big Bottom" ("Big bottom drive me out of my mind / How can I leave this behind?") that evince a juvenile and sexist perspective toward women (Plantinga, "Gender"). The film's satirical correction of a kind of pretentious hypermasculinity is crystallized in the famous scene in which the band member Derek (Harry Shearer) continually sets off alarms at an airport security checkpoint, until he feels obligated to shame-facedly remove the tinfoil-wrapped cucumber he had tucked in his jeans.

And so we come full circle. The mock documentary, as a kind of fictional screen story, does not refer to the actual world by asserting that its particulars actually exist, as a documentary would. Derek is a fictional character, after all, as are his bandmates. Instead, mock documentaries refer to the actual world as all fictional screen stories do, in their implicit assumption that the fictional characters and situations they represent have a bearing on, relate to, and refer to the actual world. They are fictional beings and situations, but they may represent actual types. A fictional character like Spinal Tap's tongue-wagging, showboating lead guitarist, Nigel, represents a type of lead guitarist who, it is implied, actually exists. Silly interviews with the fictional band members are meant to show how an interview with a heavy-metal band might actually go. The band's sexist attitudes toward women are meant to illustrate a sexist perspective that existed in heavy-metal music of the time. Just as fantasy films presume significant correspondences to quotidian reality, so do mock documentaries.

Satire in *This Is Spinal Tap* operates in part through exaggeration. The supposed pretentiousness or sense of self-importance of heavy-metal musicians is highlighted in various scenes featuring Nigel. At one point, the fictional director of the film, Marti Di Bergi (Rob Reiner), tours Nigel's showroom of guitars he has collected. So precious are Nigel's guitars that when Di Bergi reaches out his hand to touch one, Nigel berates him and adds that he should not even look at the guitar. Later we see

Nigel at the piano, describing his music as a kind of meld of Mozart and Bach, or "Moch, really." When asked the title of the piece he currently is working on, he answers, "Lick My Love Pump." We know that Nigel is a fictional character, but we clearly see him as representative of a type. Savvy viewers understand the film's implicit criticism of that type. Many fiction films refer to the actual world in just this way.

CONCLUSION

The movies are a remarkably powerful and expressive medium of art and communication. In the final analysis, realism, fantasy, films about memories and dreams, puzzle films, screen stories with twist endings, documentaries, docudramas, and mock documentaries all rely on the work of the human imagination. As a contemporary form of storytelling, all movies are rhetorical projects that imagine alternative realities. Yet each also draws from and refers to our everyday reality, to the place where we live. None can escape the rootedness of all storytelling in human experience, in human psychology and cultural context. And the movies have the means to make that relationship between imagination and the real come alive, with a power and convincingness unequaled in the history of human communication.

ACKNOWLEDGMENTS

Sincere thanks to David Wunder, Dean for Faculty Development, the Office of Research and Scholarship at Calvin University, and Provost Cheryl Brandsen for the fellowships that allowed me to finish this book. Thanks also to my department chair, Kathi Groenendyk, for her supportive approach to the scholarly and creative endeavors of members of the Calvin University Department of Communication.

My thanks go also to Nicole Solano at Rutgers University Press for leading me through the process, to series editors Gwendolyn Audrey Foster and Winston Wheeler Dixon, and to Leslie Mitchner for initially pitching the idea to me. The suggestions of an anonymous reader were very useful in revising the manuscript.

Finally, thanks to friend and colleague Stephen Prince for connecting me with Rutgers University Press.

FURTHER READING

Andrew, J. Dudley. *The Major Film Theories*. London: Oxford UP, 1976.

Armstrong, Richard. *Understanding Realism*. London: British Film Institute, 2010.

Arnheim, Rudolf. *Film as Art*. Berkeley: U of California P, 1957.

Bazin, André. *André Bazin's New Media*. Ed. and trans. Dudley Andrew. Berkeley: U of California P, 2014.

———. *What Is Cinema? Volume I*. Trans. Hugh Gray. Berkeley: U of California P, 2004.

Bernard, Sheila Curran. *Documentary Storytelling: Making Stronger and More Dramatic Nonfiction Films*. 2nd ed. Los Angeles: Focal, 2007.

Bode, Lisa. *Making Believe: Screen Performance and Special Effects in Popular Cinema*. New Brunswick, NJ: Rutgers UP, 2017.

Bordwell, David. *Poetics of Cinema*. New York: Routledge, 2008.

Campora, Mathew. *Subjective Realist Cinema: From Expressionism to Inception*. New York: Berghahn Books, 2014.

Cavell, Stanley. *The World Viewed*. Cambridge, MA: Harvard UP, 1979. Print.

Coëgnarts, Maarten, and Peter Kravanja, eds. *Embodied Cognition and Cinema.* Leuven: Leuven UP, 2015. Print.

Cornea, Christine. *Science Fiction Cinema: Between Fantasy and Reality.* New Brunswick, NJ: Rutgers UP, 2007.

Grau, Christopher, ed. *Philosophers Explore "The Matrix."* Oxford: Oxford UP, 2005.

Hedeger, Vinzenz. *The Miracle of Realism: André Bazin and the Cosmology of Film.* Amsterdam: Amsterdam UP, 2018.

Hight, Craig. *Television Mockumentary: Reflexivity, Satire, and a Call to Play.* Manchester: Manchester UP, 2010. Print.

Humann, Heather Duerre. *Reality Simulation in Science Fiction Literature, Film, and Television.* Jefferson, NC: McFarland, 2019.

Margulies, Ivone, ed. *Rites of Realism: Essays on Corporeal Cinema.* Durham, NC: Duke UP, 2002.

Morgan, Daniel. "Rethinking Bazin: Ontology and Realist Aesthetics." *The Film Theory Reader: Debates and Arguments.* Ed. Marc Furtenau. London: Routledge, 2010. 104–30.

Mosely, Philip. *The Cinema of the Dardenne Brothers: Responsible Realism.* New York: Wallflower, 2013.

Munsterberg, Hugo. *Hugo Munsterberg on Film: The Photoplay: A Psychological Study and Other Writings.* Ed. Allan Langdale. New York: Routledge, 2001.

Papandrea, James. *From Star Wars to Superman: Christ Figures in Science Fiction and Superhero Films.* Manchester, NH: Sophia Institute P, 2017.

Perez, Gilberto. *The Material Ghost: Films and Their Medium.* Baltimore: Johns Hopkins UP, 1998.

Prince, Stephen. *Digital Cinema.* New Brunswick, NJ: Rutgers UP, 2019.

———. *Digital Visual Effects in Cinema: The Seduction of Reality.* New Brunswick, NJ: Rutgers UP, 2012.

Turvey, Malcolm. *Doubting Vision: Film and the Revelationist Tradition.* Oxford: Oxford UP, 2008.

WORKS CITED

Andrew, J. Dudley. *The Major Film Theories: An Introduction.* New York: Oxford UP, 1976. Print.

Arnheim, Rudolph. *Film as Art.* Berkeley: U of California P, 1957. Print.

Barnouw, Erik. *Documentary: A History of the Non-Fiction Film.* 2nd ed. New York: Oxford UP, 1993. Print.

Bazin, André. *What Is Cinema?* Vol. 1. Ed. and trans. Hugh Gray. Berkeley: U of California P, 1967. Print.

———. *What Is Cinema?* Vol. 2. Ed. and trans. Hugh Gray. Berkeley: U of California P, 1971. Print.

Bordwell, David. *Narration in the Fiction Film.* Madison: U of Wisconsin P, 1985. Print.

———. *Poetics of Cinema.* New York: Routledge, 2008. Print.

Bordwell, David, and Kristin Thompson. *Christopher Nolan: A Labyrinth of Linkages.* 2nd ed. Madison, WI: Irvington Way Institute P, 2019. Web.

Boyd, Brian. *On the Origin of Stories: Evolution, Cognition, and Fiction.* Cambridge, MA: Belknap P, 2009. Print.

Campora, Mathew. *Subjective Realist Cinema: From Expressionism to Inception.* New York: Berghahn Books, 2014. Print.

Carroll, Noël. *Philosophical Problems of Classical Film Theory.* Princeton, NJ: Princeton UP, 1988. Print.

Carroll, Noël. *Theorizing the Moving Image*. Cambridge: Cambridge UP, 1996. Print.

Corrigan, Timothy, and Patricia White. *The Film Experience*. 3rd ed. New York: Bedford / St. Martin's, 2012. Print.

Freud, Sigmund. *The Interpretation of Dreams*. 1899. Trans. A. A. Brill. New York: Modern Library, 1995. Print.

Gould, Steven Jay. "A Biological Homage to Mickey Mouse." *The Panda's Thumb: More Reflections on Natural History*. New York: Norton, 1992. 262–70. Print.

Grau, Christopher, ed. *Philosophers Explore "The Matrix."* Oxford: Oxford UP, 2005. Print.

Henderson, Brian. *A Critique of Film Theory*. New York: E. P. Dutton, 1980. Print.

Hogan, Patrick Colm. *The Mind and Its Stories: Narrative Universals and Human Emotion*. Cambridge: Cambridge UP, 2003. Print.

Jenkins, David. "Debra Granik: How We Made *Winter's Bone*." *Time Out London* June 2010. Web.

Kiss, Miklós, and Steven Willemsen. *Impossible Puzzle Films: A Cognitive Approach to Contemporary Complex Cinema*. Edinburgh: U of Edinburgh P, 2017. Print.

Koutsourakis, Angelos. *Rethinking Brechtian Film Theory and Cinema*. Edinburgh: Edinburgh UP, 2017. Print.

Kracauer, Siegfried. *Theory of Film: The Redemption of Physical Reality*. New York: Oxford UP, 1960. Print.

MacDowell, James. *Happy Endings in Hollywood Cinema: Cliché, Convention and the Final Couple*. Edinburgh: Edinburgh UP, 2013. Print.

McGinn, Colin. *The Power of Movies: How Screen and Mind Interact*. New York: Pantheon Books, 2005. Print.

Mitry, Jean. *The Aesthetics and Psychology of the Cinema*. Trans. Christopher King. Bloomington: Indiana UP, 2000. Print.

Morgan, Daniel. "Rethinking Bazin: Ontology and Realist Aesthetics." *The Film Theory Reader*. Ed. Marc Furstenau. New York: Routledge, 2010. 104–30. Print.

Mulvey, Laura. "Visual Pleasure and the Narrative Cinema." *Screen* 16.4 (1975): 6–18. Print.

Munsterberg, Hugo. *The Film: A Psychological Study*. 1916. New York: Dover, 1970. Print.

Nichols, Bill. *Introduction to Documentary*. 3rd ed. Bloomington: Indiana UP, 2017. Print.

Perkins, V. F. *Film as Film: Understanding and Judging Movies*. 1972. New York: Da Capo, 1993. Print.

Plantinga, Carl. "Documentary." *The Routledge Companion to Philosophy and Film*. Ed. Paisley Livingston and Carl Plantinga. New York: Routledge, 2009. 494–504. Print.

———. "Folk Psychology for Film Critics and Scholars." *Projections: The Journal for Movies and Mind*, 1.2 (Winter 2011): 28–32. Print.

———. "Gender, Power, and a Cucumber: Satirizing Masculinity in *This Is Spinal Tap*." *Documenting the Documentary*. Ed. Barry Keith Grant and Jeannette Sloniowski. Detroit: Wayne State UP, 2014. Print.

———. *Moving Viewers: American Film and the Spectator's Experience*. Berkeley: U of California P, 2009. Print.

———. *Rhetoric and Representation in Nonfiction Film*. Cambridge: Cambridge UP, 1997. Print.

———. *Screen Stories: Emotion and the Ethics of Engagement*. New York: Oxford UP, 2018. Print.

Prince, Stephen. *Digital Cinema*. New Brunswick, NJ: Rutgers UP, 2018. Print.

Rockwood, Bill. "Hollywood & History: The Debate over *JFK*." *Frontline* 19 Nov. 2013. Web.

Roscoe, Jane, and Craig Hight. *Faking It: Mock-Documentary and the Subversion of Factuality*. Manchester: Manchester UP, 2001. Print.

Ryan, Marie-Laure. *Possible Worlds, Artificial Intelligence, and Narrative Theory*. Bloomington: Indiana UP, 1991. Print.

Sacks, Oliver. "In the River of Consciousness," *New York Review of Books* 51.1 (15 Jan. 2004): 41–44. Print.

Seamon, John G. *Memory and Movies: What Films Can Teach Us about Memory*. Cambridge, MA: MIT Press, 2015. Print.

Sinnerbrink, Robert. *Cinematic Ethics: Exploring Ethical Experience through Film*. New York: Routledge, 2016. Print.

Sklar, Robert. *Movie-Made America: A Cultural History of American Movies*. Rev. ed. New York: Vintage Books, 1994. Print.

Smith, Murray. *Engaging Characters: Fiction, Emotion, and the Cinema*. Oxford, UK: Clarendon, 1995. Print.

Stadler, Jane. *Pulling Focus: Intersubjective Experience, Narrative Film, and Ethics*. New York: Continuum, 2008. Print.

Talbot, William Henry Fox. *The Pencil of Nature*. 1844–46. New York: Da Capo, 1969. Print.

Thompson, Ethan. "Comedy Verité? The Observational Documentary Meets the Televisual Sitcom." *Velvet Light Trap* 60 (Fall 2007): 63–72. Print.

Turan, Kenneth. "*Saving Private Ryan*: Soldiers of Misfortune." *LA Times* 24 July 1998. Web.

Turvey, Malcolm. "Balázs: Realist or Modernist?" *The Film Theory Reader: Debates and Arguments.* Ed. Marc Furstenau. New York: Routledge, 2010. 80–89. Print.

———. *Doubting Vision: Film and the Revelationist Tradition.* Oxford: Oxford UP, 2008. Print.

Ulaby, Neda. "On Location: The Frozen Ozarks of 'Winter's Bone.'" NPR (National Public Radio) 18 Aug. 2011. Web.

Williams, Zoe. "Why *Wonder Woman* Is a Masterpiece of Subversive Feminism." *Guardian* 5 June 2017. Web.

Zacks, Jeffrey. *Flicker: Your Brain on Movies.* New York: Oxford UP, 2015. Print.

Zunshine, Lisa. *Why We Read Fiction: Theory of Mind and the Novel.* Columbus: Ohio State UP, 2006. Print.

INDEX

ABOUT THE AUTHOR

Carl Plantinga is the Arthur H. DeKruyter Chair of Communication at Calvin University in Michigan. His books as author include *Screen Stories: Emotion and the Ethics of Engagement* (2018), *Moving Viewers: American Film and the Spectator's Experience* (2009), and *Rhetoric and Representation in Nonfiction Film* (1997). He is also the coeditor of *The Routledge Companion to Philosophy and Film* (2009) and *Passionate Views: Film, Cognition, and Emotion* (1999). He is a former president of the Society for Cognitive Studies of the Moving Image.